on the run

SPIRITUALITY FOR THE SEVENTIES

Edited by
Michael F. McCauley

THE
THOMAS
MORE
PRESS

ISBN 0-88347-042-X

Table of Contents

6   INTRODUCTION

12   THE TOP DRESSER DRAWER
     by Bruce Cook

24   EVER ANCIENT, EVER NEW
     by James Hitchcock

36   PREPARING THE GROUND
     by Sally Cunneen

50   FAITH BELONGS ON MAIN STREET
     by Douglas Roche

64   AGONIZING BUT NOT IN DESPAIR
     by Albert Miller

80   IN SEARCH OF FULFILLMENT
     by Patricia Mohs

92   TO BRIDGE THE IRRECONCILABLE
     by Max Charlesworth

106   WHERE TO BEGIN
      by John Garvey

120   BUILDING THE COMMUNITY
      by Margery Frisbie

134   THERE IS TIME, YET NOT ENOUGH
      by Desmond Fisher

144   DESPITE FRUSTRATION, PURIFICATION
      by Jerome Kerwin

156   AVOIDING VANITY FAIR
      by Rosemary Haughton

168   COLOR IT BLACK
      by Kieran Quinn

186   TO CELEBRATE THE COMMONPLACE
      by John Sprague

198   RUNNING . . . WITH A LITTLE HELP
      by Jane Hughes

212   HANGING IN . . . WITH PASCAL AND THE NEW YORK TIMES
      by John Deedy

226   LIVING WITH THE TENSIONS
      by Robert Nowell

INTRODUCTION

IT'S RATHER DIFFICULT TO TALK ABOUT A SPIRITUAL LIFE IN
these times. The very phrase, "spiritual life," connotes other
worlds, other times, forgotten rituals, compulsory holiness,
pseudo-asceticism. Ignatius Loyola and his Method for Contemplation is a mere memory for some and a bizarre anach-
ronism for most. Many Catholics have not prayed—privately
—in years. And of that number virtually no one has admitted to it lately. There are just too many other, more important things to accomplish during a lifetime.

Of course, it is true that all the familiar formulas get
token exposure at wakes and the like. And on those rare
occasions when some pious priest whose prayer life just
isn't "contemporary" begins a sonorous, monotone recitation of The Rosary "for the repose of the soul of . . ."
shiftings and mumblings and bewildered expressions now
accompany the time-honored Hail Marys rather than the
enthusiastic devotion of previous generations.

That something is missing from what we used to call the
"spiritual life" is obvious. The real problem, however, is not
that the prayers and indulgences and holy hours and rosary
rallies and meditational pamphlets have disappeared from

the lives of most people except fundamentalists. The crisis—and some authors are calling it the "crisis of the seventies," the aftermath of the death of God and the disillusionment of the secular city—now arises from the lack of practices to replace the rituals, devotions and prayers that formerly characterized personal spiritual life.

Perhaps this failure to replace what was discarded with a contemporary approach to meditation, prayer and the "life of the spirit" was occasioned by the reforming church. The Council has been blamed for a great many things; why not blame the Council for a diminished prayer life. It might even be true that a number of Catholics resorted to the new-found freedoms of do-it-yourself spirituality as a result of the Council. They quickly eliminated all semblance of the "old disciplines" in favor of a new social fervor, an enlightened pragmatism that preached *do* now what you only *prayed* for in the past.

Then, too, Catholics in the seventies are a busy people. In fact, at times it seems that the best way to impress friends and elicit the admiration of new acquaintances is to proclaim loudly (and somewhat hurriedly) that we are "very busy." Implicit in this ploy is the attitude that the busier you are, the better you are—an idle mind is now, somehow, more than the devil's workshop. And God forbid that a person should stop doing or running and just *being*. No; instead one hears protests of apology and perhaps a bit of self-conscious (but nonetheless real to those who adopt this lifestyle) guilt: "I'm not doing anything right now. . . ." And being so busy hardly allows time to be spiritual or to reflect or to just contemplate where our lives have gone, what the future holds, what demands the Lord makes.

Perhaps it was an accident; perhaps it was intentional that private prayer and the spiritual life and all those things good Catholics did when they were not "hearing Mass" but were just being "good Catholics" (uttering ejaculations to get them through another day) disappeared so quickly and quietly and unnoticed from the daily lives of many. But whatever the reason, large numbers of modern Catholics do not take the time to reflect on their lives, the gospel, their faith. And yet there are those who feel vaguely uneasy about the void, the loss of spirituality.

Curiously enough, among those who are concerned about their own lack of spirituality are the sometimes caustic, almost alienated Catholics. A few still go to Sunday mass almost regularly, out of a sense of inquisitiveness, hoping each time that the homily and ceremony will "get better." Yet even this is not enough. They have often argued with friends and priests and themselves that "to work is to pray." Yet now, after years of emphasizing the work and sliding on the prayer, some are confessing that what Benedict meant was evidently more complicated than they had anticipated. Somehow they became entangled in that old "the busier I am, the more I'm praying" ruse that we seem so susceptible to. In fact, not a few were encouraged by their newly liberated priests who recommended a life of action but counseled against prayer: "I don't pray; why should you? Prayer is irrelevant. Prayer is medieval. Prayer is [the real clincher] immature." They merely reinforced all the suspicions of the skeptics. And if Father doesn't pray, why bother? Let's be about the business of living and the prayers will follow from the action.

However, all that was the "secularity of the sixties." Many of those sixties things that people had been doing-praying have turned out to be less fulfilling than promised. It's not that the action-pray-ers feel guilty about not having the kind of spiritual life that meant rosary-saying and devotional exercises and private prayer. No; for them, formula prayers were meaningless and so they just stopped praying that way. The difficulty is that the activism and other meaningful concerns that were part of sixties doing-praying are not really producing the desired effect. Somewhere, the secular activists changed gears and began meditating and contemplating. A number even began to talk about their "spiritual life" and did not feel any need to apologize. Now there is a desire for something more. Interior peace, a sense of selflessness, a spiritual communion with God and men is at least as important as jumping headlong into the alienation of society with all those doing-praying programs for revitalization.

On the other hand, there are those Catholics who never abandoned their prayers and spiritual exercises. They have been praying, since childhood, and are praying still. They have a spiritual life. They have kept abreast of Vatican II changes, read with satisfaction the spiritual writers of the day (Thomas Merton, Simone Weil, Michel Quoist, Hubert Van Zeller), and often reread the classics. (Saints John of the Cross and Teresa of Avila—two giants of the spiritual life—have regained positions of importance with Catholics concerned about their own spirituality.) Their spiritual lives are vital and rewarding and inspiring.

Assuming that increasing numbers of Catholics feel the need for a spiritual life of some sort and the total dissatisfaction with past practices and the current void, what's to be done? Evidently there are Catholics who have a mature spiritual life—who have "put away the things of children" and can pray as adults aware of what's happening in the world. And when we hear about people who have maintained a spiritual lifestyle and find inspiration and motivation from prayer two questions immediately arise: (1) How can they possibly do it? There is not enough time in the day to accomplish all the things we *have* to do, let alone a few that we might *want* to do. (2) What kinds of "spiritual" things do these people do? What is involved in an effective spiritual life? Can I do it?

If there is to be a spirituality for the seventies it will undoubtedly come from people most involved in the lifestyle of the seventies—many of whom have family as well as professional obligations and yet find time, or *make* time, to have some kind of spiritual life. We have asked seventeen laypeople that very pointed question, "How do you do it?" All have replied in a very personal way—some of the essays which follow are autobiographical; some appear to be excerpted from diaries—explaining what "spiritual activities" are meaningful for the authors, what steps they have taken to insure that their very busy lifestyles include some form of meditation, reflection, prayer. But most important are those insights into the meaning of the spiritual life that these seventeen people come to—their relationship to themselves, to others and to God.

Although some of our authors are not completely satisfied with their current spiritual lives they have not given up; they continue to search for more effective methods. Some utilize "secular" approaches to prayer and meditation; some have explored Eastern methods of contemplation; for most, involvement in the lives of others continues to be effective. All have found ways to revitalize their spirituality—ways to pray and even contemplate despite increasing demands on their lives. It is not easy, to be sure. Disenchantment, distraction, just plain weariness often overcome any interest in things spiritual. A Teilhardian conviction of the inherent spiritual value of the things of this world underscores the dedication of each. And yet there remains mature, adult concern for what previous generations called the things of the spirit.

At times, it may seem that we are constantly running at breakneck speeds, trying to cram twenty-six hours of activity into a twenty-four hour day. Quite often, all of our running results merely in trying to keep up, trying to stay in place. There must be a way to sustain a real spiritual life—even if we must do it on the run. To this end the following is dedicated.

Michael F. McCauley

THE TOP
DRESSER DRAWER

A *staff writer for the* National Observer, *BRUCE COOK has written for a number of publications, among them* Commonweal, The Nation, The Critic, U.S. Catholic, *and* The New Leader. *He has published two books,* The Beat Generation *and* Listen to the Blues. *Mr. Cook, his wife and their three children live in a suburb of* Washington, D.C.

by Bruce Cook

THE GIDEONS CERTAINLY KNEW WHAT THEY WERE DOING. THE group, more properly known as the Christian Commercial Men's Association of America, is known to most of us for one thing and one thing only: putting Bibles in hotel rooms. Why there? Why not hospital rooms? Why not prison cells? Why not a hundred other places?

Well, if you've spent much time in hotel rooms you wouldn't have to ask. What awful hours those can be! I'm not talking about boredom. If that were all there was to it, you wouldn't need a Bible; you could get along with a mystery, or a copy of *Playboy*, or by staring all night at that blinking, blue-lit glass screen opposite the bed. But boredom isn't half of it. That's just a prelude, a precondition to the awful gut-wrenching loneliness that soon sets in. So what else can you do?

You call home, and that makes you feel better for about the length of the phone call—and then it makes you feel worse as soon as you hang up. Soon you're so homesick and restless that you know you're not going to get to sleep that night unless you drug yourself with booze. And so, unless you've been realistic and foresighted enough to bring along a bottle in your suitcase, down you go to the cocktail lounge in the lobby, or across the street to where that sign is flashing on the corner. Naturally you have too much to drink—that was the idea, wasn't it? You get back at last to the hotel room, flop into bed and still you can't sleep, or—even worse—the booze keeps you under for a few hours and about 4:30 or 5:00 A.M. you bolt awake, feeling awful, hating yourself, in sudden spiritual panic remembering all the rotten things you've ever said or done your whole life long. If you're old enough to have friends now dead you remember them and hope they remember you. You may miss one terribly, or think that if you'd only been a little better to another he might not have committed suicide. And so. . . .

After a while, when those four walls have pressed in on you long enough and the room is knee-deep in layers of anxiety and despondency, there is nowhere to go but to the top drawer in the dresser where, if you're lucky, you find a Gideon Bible. What do you read? One of the Gospels is best—you can go through Mark in not much more than an hour, and just *reading* it helps. The Psalms are good, and some of St. Paul's letters are okay. But take my advice, and in such times of stress stay away from the Book of Revelation. It's too scary.

That's right—the Book of Revelation, not the Apocalypse—for all the Gideon Bibles I've ever seen have been the King James version. And frankly, I prefer it so. As a matter of fact, since you can't always count on finding a Bible in that top dresser drawer (the Gideons can't get them everywhere, I guess, and people must take them like towels, too), I've bought a little one to take with me in the suitcase along with that bottle of booze. It's a King James version. I've got an old Douay-Reims around the house, and the new Oxford translation, and I suppose they are okay, but not really right for the kind of doomsday reading I've just described. Why not? Well, I could make some appeal to the magnificent 17th-Century prose of the King James and suggest that the slight strangeness of the language is right for such occasions: When we converse with the Infinite, we don't expect to be answered in a plain style. Which may be true enough, but the more fundamental reason, I suspect, is that I prefer it because the King James is the one I grew up with.

I'm a convert to Catholicism. Who can say why? It may have had something to do with my attitude to the Methodism in which I was brought up—let that read, "adolescent rebellion." It may, and probably does, have a lot to do with the fact that I went to a Catholic university and found much to admire in the way that people I met there took their faith (not to mention the Faith) with admirable seriousness. And it almost certainly had a lot to do with the fact that I married a Catholic and submitted to the sort of shameful blackmail that people submitted to in those days—signing a document, worth utterly nothing except in ecclesiastical court, promising not to practice birth control and to bring up the children according to the precepts of good old Superchurch. So I must have figured I might as well go whole hog and be a sort of Catholic since I had to act like one anyway. Do I sound bitter? I'm not. I've had a good marriage. I like my kids. And I have been treated to some very interesting internal conflicts that I might other-wise never have had. No regrets.

But down deep, obviously, I'm still more than somewhat a Protestant. Those orgies of self-reproach of mine that I call the Dooms, the hotel room crises that come up from time to time, are essentially reversions to my Protestant past. That they come as they do is proof, I'm afraid, that my spiritual life is sporadic, haphazard, and a bit desperate in nature. It is, in this way, anything but unique. Although not everyone endures these Dooms of mine (and lucky for them), most of us today tend to neglect spirituality on any sort of regular basis until, finally, we no longer can. Oh, we go to church on Sunday, though we often tune out the sermons and with good reason. We pray when we think of it, which is not often enough. And if we do much spiritual reading, it is not because we go to the usual, acceptable sources of inspiration—the Bible, traditional writings such as *Imitation of Christ,* or to modern writers such as Michel Quoist. No, it is because we have widened the definition and manage to draw moral and spiritual lessons from what some would consider quite unlikely places—from fiction, histories, biographies, even the daily newspaper. Properly read, there is no more instructive moral document—"O vanity of vanities!"—than the daily newspaper, although it, too, can lead some to despair.

But my occasional spiritual crises, and the equivalent experiences of others who live in just such a slapdash state, prove something else quite important: That the spiritual life may be neglected, but it cannot be ignored. Just when you think you may have left that dimension completely, you come crashing through that remarkably thin tissue we consider day-to-day reality and find yourself quite suddenly up against the starker, harder, more abrasive stuff that is spiritual reality. Or perhaps better put, given a long enough line, you may start cutting fancy figures and forget we are all tethered. And what happens when you get too far out?

Why, you find yourself dumped rather quickly flat on your ass. Which posture, incidentally—bowed head and bended knee notwithstanding—is the one most common for spiritual exercise today. Perhaps it was always so.

Not that I'm knocking day-to-day reality, mind you. Since I've already offered my involvement in it and concern for it as an excuse for my neglect of the spiritual, that would be awfully disingenuous of me, wouldn't it? And I couldn't do that anyway because quite frankly I am fascinated by it. The physical reality of people—what they say, what they do —has always fascinated me. That, I suppose, is fundamentally how I happen to spend so much time in hotel rooms: I'm a writer by craft, and a journalist by trade. And I can think of no other pursuit that could possibly feed my insatiable curiosity about human beings as does this one. That, I guess, is why once firmly into it, I have never thought seriously about changing to some less dislocating occupation. Just when I might begin to do so, I am given the chance to go off someplace and meet somebody I have always wanted to.

They call this meeting an interview, and it is a rare sort of social experience. It has nothing to do with getting friendly with the people you interview—that doesn't enter into it at all. No, it is a sort of heightened conversation in which the interviewer has a license to ask almost any question, and the interviewee has an obligation to try to answer truthfully— people try to do that more and more, I'm convinced of it.

What sort of person might one want to meet under such circumstances? Well, ideally, someone like Malcolm Muggeridge. I went to Europe a few years ago determined to interview him, having sent letters ahead hoping to arrange it.

What attracted me to him, first of all, was professional admiration. For whatever else Muggeridge is today—controversialist, television personality, professional crank—he is certainly a journalist's journalist. There is no better writer of English prose around. No professional observer has a sharper eye for human absurdities than he does. And nobody deals with them quite as mercilessly and wittily as he can. As a journalist he is all that I would want to be and two or three times what I might ever become.

But he is something more. Malcolm Muggeridge is a practicing Christian at a time and in a way in which it is unfashionable to be so. There is, God knows, nothing trendy about his brand of Christianity. It is infused with the old puritan English spirit, the love of controversy and the loathing of compromise. And while he is known through all of England and much of America for his firm stand for Christianity, it cannot be said that it has added to his popularity, especially in intellectual circles. Of all this, of course, he is keenly aware but cares nothing. "The commonest opinion," he writes in *Jesus Rediscovered*, a collection of his writings on his encounter with Christianity, "is that with advancing years I have gone soft and become a bore—two perfectly plausible judgments. . . ."

I had read that book of his, and it had meant a good deal to me, partly because it was an affirmation of faith from a man I already respected, but more importantly because it had come to me when my own faith badly needed affirming. There I was at the very bottom of my post-Vatican II depression, and it was ironic, to say the least, that I hoped to be brought out of it by a very conservative Christian, one largely out of sympathy with what I regarded as the authentic spirit of renewal in the church. But my meeting with him did just that. It seemed to bring me closer to something fundamental, something we all share.

Yes, I did get that meeting with him. We had our interview. Most of what he told me he had expressed elsewhere —we have only so many answers in us, after all—as I covered the usual wide range of topics with him. But on the matter of what he considered his conversion to Christianity we did dwell a bit. Somebody I know had seen a program that he had done on Lourdes for BBC and had suggested to me that he seemed so profoundly affected by what he had seen there at the Shrine that it may have been instrumental in bringing him to Christianity—and if so, my informant had wondered, why was he not a Catholic? Muggeridge told me that yes, of course, he had been affected by the faith he had seen displayed at Lourdes—"Who could not be?" But as far as its being the sort of Damascus-road experience I implied, probably not. What then? Well, there had been three programs he had done from the Holy Land that had touched him profoundly, given him a feeling of reality and certainty about Jesus Christ and the Gospel story that had not left him. But even that had not brought about a dramatic change. It had been a gradual thing, he said, a lifelong journey for him, from nonbelieving to believing. There had been some reading along the way, though, that had helped, and then he mentioned Simone Weil. Had I read her? No. Muggeridge said he thought I would find her worth my attention.

I had heard of her, of course. A French Jew who had done brilliantly as a student in Philosophy at the Ecole Normale Superieure, she had, in fact, been a classmate of

Simone de Beauvoir's and Jean-Paul Sartre's and had finished just above both of them in class standings. (She appears as a character in Sartre's novel *The Age of Reason*.)
Having been raised an agnostic, as Muggeridge had been,
she proceeded, quite on her own, to move closer and closer
to Christianity—so close, in fact, that she made an eloquent
and regretful apology to her spiritual counselor, Father
Perrin, that she could not become a Catholic. (In men-
tioning Simone Weil, pre-eminently the convert who did
not enter the church, Malcolm Muggeridge said much to
me indirectly about his own hesitations regarding Catholicism—so much that I could not begin to summarize it all
here.) She died during World War II, though not violently;
she was no less a casualty of her time than the thousands of
French Jews who were deported and executed by the Nazis.

When she died at the age of 34, she left behind her
a considerable body of writing—much, if not most of it,
having to do with her journey to Christianity. It was this
that Muggeridge was commending to me. The next day, in
London, I picked up an English paperback copy of *Waiting
on God*, by Simone Weil. I have kept it, read it, and reread it a number of times. I don't know, however, that I can
legitimately consider this as spiritual reading, or include my
interest in her as a bona fide part of my spiritual life. My
interest in her is partly biographical; too much of my attention is directed *at* her and not enough perhaps at God
through her, which seems the more proper attitude for spiritual exercise. And as for my interest in her writing—well,
she gives me a lot to chew on. But she never lost the philoso-
pher's attitude of mind, and most of what she has written
are quite closely reasoned attempts to solve philosophical

problems to do with religion. What she writes is not theology. It is certainly not intended as spiritual writing. It is religious philosophy. Nevertheless some of it is so beautifully and epigrammatically expressed that it might be possible to quote a few things out of context to give some idea of the quality of her thought.

From *Waiting on God,* on not allowing oneself to become overly subjective in one's spiritual life:

> It is not my business to think about myself. My business is to think about God. It is for God to think about me.

On intellectual adventuring:

> Christ likes us to prefer truth to him because, before being Christ, he is truth. If one turns aside from him to go towards the truth, one will not go far before falling into his arms.

From her *Notebooks:*

> God alone possesses the right to prefer men to God.

And:

> Work—this is always man acting as a counterweight to the universe. And the pain of work is transformed into passion when man works without personal motives and incentives.
> But what happens when man works under the lash?

That last is representative of a special area of her thought. She wrote with great authority on work. She knew better than most the reality of physical labor. After taking her diploma she worked for a period in the Renault factory in

order to know better the people her friends discussed in the
abstract as the "proletariat." She went to pains in her
writings on work to demonstrate how devotion to God
might be maintained through and during labor of all sorts.
Most helpful to me personally, though, has been a little
essay entitled, "Reflections on the Right Use of School
Studies," which Simone Weil wrote to inspire the students
of Father Perrin when he was Superior of the Dominicans
of Montpellier. What the essay says is stated most succinctly in a *Notebook* entry from which it was developed:

> Studies and faith. Since prayer is but attention in
> its pure form, and since studies constitute a gymnastic
> of the attention, it follows that every school exercise
> should be a refraction of spiritual life. But this depends
> on the use of a method. A certain way of doing a Latin
> translation, a certain way of doing a problem in ge-
> ometry—and not just any sort of way—these consti-
> tute a gymnastic of the attention calculated to render
> it more fitted for prayer.

"Prayer is but attention in its pure form"—that suggests to
me that what I lack is the proper sort of attention. Too
many distractions. So that the fragmented, jumpy quality
of my life, as that of so many others, makes me less able to
direct my concentration where and how it should be directed.

Difficult? Of course it is. Nobody said it would be easy.
Malcolm Muggeridge even suggested it might take a lifetime to do the job right. Well, a lifetime is all I have—is
all any one of us has to try.

In the meantime, to be realistic, I shall probably continue about as I have for years to come—trying a little harder to develop my attention in that attitude of prayer, perhaps eventually getting a little better at it as time goes by. I'll probably keep right on suffering the Dooms every now and then, waking up hung over in hotel rooms, and in sudden spiritual panic, grabbing desperately for that Bible in the top dresser drawer.

EVER ANCIENT,
EVER NEW

A *native of St. Louis—where he and his family now reside —* JAMES HITCHCOCK *has been a professor of history at St. Louis University since 1966. He is the author of* The Decline and Fall of Radical Catholicism *and* The Recovery of the Sacred. *His articles have appeared in countless journals including the* New York Times Magazine, The Yale Review, Commonweal *and* The Christian Century. *Currently, he is a columnist for* The Critic.

by James Hitchcock

PERHAPS LIKE MOST PEOPLE IN THIS AGE, I FIND MYSELF living to a great extent off spiritual capital accumulated earlier, in a time which at least seemed more settled, certain, and tranquil, more conducive to inner spiritual development than the present. Although I sense that in some ways I have "grown in grace" in the past ten years, I have even more the sense of resting on an unseen and often only barely felt foundation which has its weak places but on the whole has proven remarkably strong and sustains me in situations I might not otherwise survive.

The familiar metaphor of the foundation in the spiritual life easily gives way to that of the replenishing stream, and in terms of this shift I am conscious also that my soul's life is continually irrigated from obscure subterranean sources, sometimes in bare trickles, occasionally in bracing gushes, over which I appear to have little control but which are the accumulation of waters from earlier and heavier rains.

In part this is probably true of everyone, in that the religious sense as developed in childhood and impressionable adolescence doubtlessly shapes adult perceptions. Insofar as I can analyze my own case, I think that a sensitivity to religious symbol and a sense of religious awe, stimulated in childhood, are the most important prerequisites for an adult religious life. Everything which comes later is in some sense a variation on this.

In part, also, it appears to be a function of the times which, despite the recent revival of interest in religious disciplines and prayer, do not seem highly conducive to religious development. In all probability the foundations of this development have to be laid in times of relative tranquillity, although stress and turmoil can be, judging from the lives of the saints, occasions of growth. We do not, however, live in an age which is particularly sympathetic even to the idea of the spiritual life, and our age increasingly seems to impose, with iron-willed system, that greatest of all enemies of true spirituality—distraction, the constant filling of one's mind and one's daily life with quantities of information, ceaseless entertainment, repeated invitations to action and involvement, so as to make any concern with the inner life seem in fact a luxury. At the same time the unsuitability of the spirit of the age should not be exaggerated. John Donne, writing 350 years ago, might have been describing most of us:

> I throw myself down in my chamber, and I call in and invite God and his Angels thither, and when they are there I neglect God and his Angels, for the noise of a fly, for the rattling of a coach, for the whining of a door. I talk on, in the same posture of praying, eyes lifted up, knees bowed down, as though I prayed to God. And, if God or his Angels should ask me when I thought last of God in that prayer, I cannot tell. Some-

times I find that I forgot what I was about, but when
I began to forget I cannot tell. A memory of Yesterday's
pleasures, a fear of tomorrow's dangers, a straw under
my knee, a noise in mine ear, a light in mine eye, an
anything, a nothing, a fancy, a chimera in my brain
troubles me in my prayer. So certainly is there nothing
in spiritual things perfect in this world.

The perennial relevance of Donne's account, along with the
fact that, as far as we can tell, he was a man of genuine
prayer and deep devotion after all, helps explain my conviction that classical models of spirituality have not been
superseded and that, if they are in temporary eclipse, this
is due less to them and more to the immense psychological
pressures brought against them in this age, pressures which
paradoxically serve merely to reemphasize their importance.

A vital spirituality seems to depend first of all on the per-
sistence of some kind of vision, which may fade in and out
but which is never wholly absent. With such a vision various formalized approaches to spirituality may be more or
less helpful; without it they are useless. How such a vision
comes about remains mysterious. For myself, I am highly
conscious of what Francois Mauriac describes as a "sense
of invisible reality" present from childhood on. For most
believers such a vision is probably formed quite early, but
the phenomenon of adult conversions is sufficiently familiar
to demonstrate that it need not be.

This vision is, for me, ultimately ineffable. Phrases like
"Union with Christ," "the majesty of God," "the presence
of mystery," "penetrating the veil of appearances," "the
nearness of eternity," "the love of God," and many others

resonate with the sense of invisible realities which I find ebbs and flows within me. What precisely such phrases mean, I cannot say. That they denote something more real than newspaper headlines or even the most acute insights of modern "secular" men, I am certain. The riveting power of sanctity, as a distinct and recognizable Christian category, seems to me more compelling than any merely human heroism. The most attractive saints—Catherine of Siena, Philip Neri, Vincent de Paul, Charles de Foucauld, and others—seem to reveal in their persons a profound dimension of reality not found in secular heroes no matter how courageous or devoted.

Religion seems to me primarily an esthetic thing, not in the sense that it is a self-fulfilling experience or a search for pleasure but in the sense that it is, ideally, an almost unfree response to overwhelming beauty. It is, as Baron von Hügel succinctly stated, pure adoration. C. S. Lewis insisted that there is in Christianity some idea of God as the "Great Interferer," and no aspect of Christianity has been more a stumbling block to enlightened modern men. But God is first of all the Interferer not in a moral or physical sense but as an overpowering reality who cannot be ignored, who intrudes himself into self-contained human existence in the way that the ocean or a Beethoven symphony intrudes. Away from either, we may find their memories dimming, their power growing doubtful. In their proximity again, we realize that we have been living in a deliberately circumscribed and impoverished world. More and more I find music the purest expression of religion and the greatest stimulus to devotion. (The fact that I am largely devoid of technical and scholarly competence about music probably enhances this experience.)

The tension of "vertical" and "horizontal" in religion has exercised far too much influence over recent theological and ascetical discussion. The "correct" position is obvious enough—the true Christian must be both God-oriented and man-oriented. Those who are truly both are probably fairly well along the road to sainthood. I confess to the discouraging sense that such a balance is rare in actual people, that most serious Christians are tipped either one way or the other, although never, of course, completely. Those with a taste and a capacity for contemplation do seem able to shut out a good deal of the world, to prune away distractions and conflicting demands on their time and attention, while the social apostles often appear to have little interest in devotion and a strong propensity for losing themselves in worldly events. The exceptions are, mercifully, sufficiently numerous to indicate the possibility, but not so numerous as to permit complacency.

I find that I cannot be a "secular man" because the reality which is formulated in the doctrine of the Mystical Body of Christ in effect gives the believer special glasses, somewhat like those we wore for a brief while at "3-D" movies, which reveal new dimensions to the world and to human existence. On one level I am very concerned with the concrete texture of life and with its preservation, and few things seem clearer to me than that most of the forces of modern life, whether of the "right" or the "left," seek to destroy that texture. Yet in another sense I find myself believing, often, that this does not matter, that one's sexual, racial, national, professional, or familial identities are ultimately absorbed into the unity of Christ. I am at least a moderately "political" person, in that I care about society and human culture. Yet I also sometimes think public events are of small consequence, that victories and defeats, achievements and failures, are ultimately cancelled out by eternity.

It seems to me altogether appropriate that Christianity should be full of paradoxes which approach being contradictions, and it is one of the most distressing features of the contemporary church that so much effort is being expended to resolve these paradoxes in a rational and "secular" way. We are in the world but not of it. What we do on earth matters greatly and matters not at all. God desires our prayers but has no need of them. He is all-just and all-merciful. Christ was fully God and fully man. It seems to me that nowhere has the inherently paradoxical nature of human existence been better recognized than in the fundamental Christian dogmas and in the basic, ingrained attitudes of traditional spirituality. ("Pray as though everything depends on God; work as though everything depends on you.")

One of the most profound "religious" experiences I have had (less common now that the Church has become so factionalized) is of Mass in a large city church at rush hour on a holyday, with crowds of the most diverse people gathered together to participate in a great transcendent act of worship which leaves our differences unaffected (we need not even greet each other or smile; we are in a hurry to get home in any case) while subsuming them into the eternal and the infinite. Many have come out of a sense of obligation, but they come reverently nonetheless. Our humanity is all too apparent, but briefly at least we are made aware of our divinity as well.

Paradoxically also, the pure beauty, the unbounded love, the perfect freedom which are the ends of our spiritual life seem attainable only through a measure of asceticism and self-denial, the acceptance of discipline, the adoption of a regimen. Great art is never either created or apprehended solely through spontaneity; training and discipline are required, and also experience. Prayer never seems more meaningless than when I have neglected it for a while, or more nourishing than when I have forced myself to practice it for a few days. The talk about introducing Catholics to an "adult spirituality" seems to me often to miss the point. It is precisely the mark of childhood to be fresh, spontaneous, and indiscriminate in enthusiasms, to care nothing for the future, to acquire and drop new loves daily, to rely on "the spirit blowing where it will." The adult learns to discern the real from the chimeric, to limit enthusiasms to what is digestible, above all to adopt methods and strategies which prolong pleasures and commitments, to live in a sense according to rules. The adult recognizes that the waning of first emotions does not betoken necessarily the waning of commitment.

It is perhaps the central genius of Catholicism that it has devised so many ways to prolong the effects of spontaneous insight long after the insight itself has become obscured. That is the principal point of dogma, of fixed liturgy, of behavioral rules, of guides to the spiritual life. Catholicism has been accused of being a religion of rote and of blind obedience. Where it fails to take inner root in its adherents, it does in fact become this. However, its aim is something different. Catholicism rather teaches that, if the sincere individual undertakes to live a certain way of life, to follow a certain designated path, he or she will come finally to the clear place in the forest or, to vary the metaphor, to the crown of the hill from which the Promised

Land can be glimpsed in the distance. The discipline precedes the understanding and, once the understanding is attained, also sustains it.

What historical Catholicism in effect does is to seize upon deep spiritual insights, moments of overwhelming grace, and crystallize them. The most important of these crystallizations are in the liturgy, and the liturgy remains for me the culmination, in a very tangible and personal way, of the life of the spirit. I simultaneously approach liturgy in an "objective" way—as the actual celebration of a divine rite whose true meaning is mystical—and in a "subjective" way —I am perhaps overly sensitive to the way in which liturgy is celebrated. The recitation of the Divine Office by monks and nuns, the smoke of incense rising to heaven, the performance of prescribed rituals, all seem to me to have objective religious validity; it is good that they occur, apart from the personal state of those who do them. At the same time I recognize that the symbolic power of liturgy can be greatly enhanced and obscured by, among other things, the style of celebration. On the subjective side the reform of the liturgy has for me largely diminished this power, as I believe it has also for many other people.

In his autobiography, Thomas Merton records that when he first thought of turning to religion as a young man, he began by going to the rather drab and uninspiring little Protestant church he had dropped out of years before. It was, he said, as though God wanted him to climb back up the way he fell. Like many people, I gave up a good many of the traditional devotions after the Second Vatican Council, not in order to become "secular" but in order to discover a "higher" kind of spirituality. Gradually I have been recognizing the barely concealed pride in that action, which perhaps as much as anything else has prevented the flowering of that hoped for higher life. I have come to realize, as Pascal and others have often pointed out, that simple things like kneeling to pray, using holy water, or reciting the great traditional prayers, do make a difference. Perhaps having been away from them for a time I come to them refreshed and with a clearer view. In any case I recommend to anyone seeking the renewal of his spiritual life that he begin with a fixed and even arbitrary regime—a certain time set aside, certain prayers to be said, certain books to be read, kneeling, making the sign of the cross, etc.

In saying that I often have the feeling of living off past spiritual capital, I mean also that I now realize the importance of ingrained images, words, sentences, gestures which have been deeply rooted in the subconscious over a period of time and come to the surface unexpectedly. Phrases from the traditional liturgy, sometimes in Latin, sentences from the scripture (usually in the Douay-Reims version we heard for so long), recollections of particular works of religious art, come into the mind unbidden and, for someone still in the foothills of the spiritual life, help to make possible the fulfillment of Christ's injunction to "pray always." The secularity and spiritual dryness of many contemporary Catholics is doubtlessly related to the fact that so many powerful images from the past—verbal and inconographic —have been allowed to fade. I do not think the newer images will prove nearly so powerful; in part they are designed not to be.

Although my sense of the meaning of religion is that it is ultimately a response to great beauty, the "negative" side of faith has always seemed important to me also. The final glory is precious only because we have first fallen in the valley of tears. Concepts like "sin" and "repentance" seem to me much closer to true human reality than talk about "growth," "fulfillment," or "potential." Although I cannot follow him all the way, Martin Luther has been one of the strongest theological influences on me, in his determination that man shall first confront his own sinfulness in all its depth before he shall enjoy the comforts of salvation. The seemingly exaggerated importance which St. Augustine gives to his theft of a few pears also seems real to me, in that the moral universe I perceive is one in which small deeds, even small thoughts, can have immense personal consequences. I have always been attracted to the rather astringent, sin-conscious Gallic piety represented in recent times by Mauriac, Bernanos, and Claudel and correspondingly put off by the cheerfulness of a certain English attitude expressed by people like Chesterton and C. S. Lewis. To say that one senses in himself the capacity for every kind of sin is both self-dramatizing and probably untrue, but some approximation of this seems to me necessary for full spiritual development.

Like most Catholics, I go to confession less often than I used to, although I am not sure why. The idea of it still appeals to me. Probably the greatest problem with it, so far as I am concerned, is the discrepancy between what it promises to be and what it is, subjectively speaking—so often it turns out purely routine and perfunctory. Still, the forgiveness is pronounced and the grace imparted. At the least it is a reminder that we are constantly under God's judgment. A seminarian once said to me, "I'm a Christian to help prevent me from being myself," and that seems to me exactly right. Nothing in the "new church" seems to me more ill-conceived than the apparent general optimism about human nature which is now so pervasive. My vision of evil is of pure and unbridled egotism, and we live in an age which appears systematically to encourage this.

Most of the time I experience no particular fear of hell or desire for heaven, which is more a sign of worldliness than of advanced spirituality. I also find that my worldly desires seem to be fewer and my ability to endure disappointments greater, which are more likely to be evidences of aging than of purification. I think, however, that I am beginning to see the truth in the assertion that Christianity does not promise happiness as the world understands it, that happiness in this sense is ultimately irrelevant. In retrospect my greatest human disappointments seem to me in some ways providential, and I am sometimes surprised at the ease and subtlety with which God has seemingly guided me in ways I did not intend to go and given me tasks I did not intend to undertake.

PREPARING THE GROUND

Writer, editor and lecturer, SALLY CUNNEEN is on the editorial staff of Cross Currents. *She is the author of* Sex: Female; Religion: Catholic *and has written for a variety of Catholic publications including* Commonweal *and* America. *Currently, she is teaching English at Rockland Community College, New York.*

by Sally Cunneen

JUST BEFORE LENT A LETTER ARRIVED FROM THE EDITOR
asking for an essay on my personal spirituality. Do I dare,
knowing that nothing is clear and formulated? There is not
even a pattern. Just a vacillating will and the certainty that
"this isn't enough." Yet there are certain moments of seeing
that come as pure gift. Perhaps they could be shared.

On the first Sunday in Lent, the Cardinal's letter was read
outlining regulations. Surely it was too Skinnerian; we were
advised to give up food and drink, especially drink; it was
suggested we might help our alcoholic problem with this
sacrifice, thus improving relationships with our long-suffer-
ing family. Yet at dinner tonight a journalist friend and
neighbor told of men who have been alcoholics and given
up alcohol for Lent, thereby satisfying themselves that they
were not alcoholics and making life a permanent hell for
their families.

We were also told to be examples to the community at
large, which is going down the headlong path to paganism.
We were strongly urged to attend daily mass. We were, in
truth, urged to be the best sheep we could be, as distin-
guished from the goats around us.

I need help from the church but this is not it. I feel as if I am back in St. Sebastian's in the nineteen-thirties. WE and THEY. External actions will make you pious and help you show your irreligious neighbors the way.

But the real struggle is with myself. Giving up alcohol (which would be a good idea, since I'm putting on weight and, besides, it exaggerates my allergies) is just a part of trying to live as the person I am, instead of trying to blot out awareness. A more difficult task for me is the one I flubbed at dinner when I took my oldest son's snapping as a personal insult, wasting emotion and damaging delicate relationships.

Only after a walk alone outside did I realize that his remark had not been directed precisely against me, but only as I fit into inevitably unsatisfactory social and economic presuppositions of life, the very ones he must struggle to improve. I fell into the trap through my own automatic pride, and probably helped confuse the very perception I would want sharp and clear in him. Maybe at least I have learned to try to be still, to listen. *Not to jump* even when vanity feels pricked. People who are growing are so complex; they go back and forward in time, forming themselves, and nothing is more demanding or exciting than being involved in such growth.

****

A cold and sunny Monday with March crocuses so I can do something for Joe's mother at last. I haven't been able to see her or talk to her since she had a stroke a month ago. She wanders back and forth to her childhood, calls Mary

Elisabeth, the only one she wants nearby, and invokes all the names from long-dead sisters to cousins far away. The worst of it is, she is fearful. At 89, her children and grand-children grown, lovely and kind even in dependence though she always loved to give, she has no security. She has nothing but worries for all the children who are gone and for the unknown future.

Only Mary Elisabeth can comfort her, so she rushes from her job as insurance salesman to comfort Mom. She is exhausted at the physical and psychological drain, but superb as always. Perhaps for her it takes some of the frustration out of all the changes in the world, especially the church, all the opportunities not taken because of fiscal and family responsibilities, just to be so totally needed and busy—if she doesn't collapse.

"Is there anything I can do?" I ask ineptly.

"I think a crocus in bloom might cheer her up," Mary Elisabeth replies, and I know she is right. So I dig up gravel and dirt, find an outcast marmalade jar that's the right shape, and select a not-quite-budding yellow crocus surrounded by its star-shaped white-striped leaves. This is sharing at its simplest level: no words, no caresses, just the meaning I cannot express, know I could not convey, but is there in the black-moist earth, the radiant bud. May God have mercy on us all.

****

Off to an ecumenical meeting, I am sitting at the coffee counter in Kennedy airport, observing Japanese business-men, young men with rakish moustaches, a man in overalls

on a ladder screwing in light blubs above a row of tubs filled
with pyramided plastic flowers. The twisted steel sculpture
on the walls matches the sandwiches standing on end,
bunched together in triangular cardboard-cellophane wrap-
pers on the shelf.

Unexpectedly I am reminded of my parents, both dead
for over twenty years. Is it because I remember that when
they took me traveling I would have suffered through the
same scene? I was tense then, fighting them as well as the
surroundings, all tied up in the struggle for identity. Now I
enjoy it all, even the sterile airport decor I would have re-
sisted then with more energy than it deserved. Perhaps
Chaplin and Tati have mediated the products of impersonal modernism for me.

Worse, I would have avoided the human variety around
the counter as the young man opposite me does, nervous
eyes setting barriers against chance meetings with other
travelers. At the time I could not have done otherwise. Yet
my parents would have seen it much as I do now. Their
attitude then would have varied from mine today only in
an easier acceptance of the sterility as a sign of progress.

I would like to tell them I've changed, but they have
gone. My eyes fill with tears as I sip the coffee handed me by
an outwardly pleasant but reserved waitress wearing her first
name pinned to her blouse. A short middle-aged man settles
in next to me and asks in a kindly Scottish burr: "Molly,
m'dear, what goodies do y'have for me this morning?" The
waitress freezes and hands him a menu.

"Any honey in those little plastic things?" he asks dis-
armingly.

"No sir," she replies, "just grape jelly and strawberry jam."

"I knew I should have brought some with me," he muses, gloomily reviewing the menu.

While one part of me wonders, how could he carry the honey, the rest feels: *it is all so beautiful*. I owe my parents so much. Now that I have children as old as I was then, I realize how much my parents loved me, hoped for me, ennobled me. As a child I had enjoyed my mother's tale of her visits to *two* shrines of St. Anne, asking particularly for *me* to be born. As a girl I thrived on my father's insistence that women could and should do anything they wanted, and at least as well as a man. His admiration for Margaret Bourke-White, Amelia Earhart and Claire Booth Luce was unfeigned; his expectations for his daughters were limited only by the freedom of choice he felt was theirs.

How I would love to translate some of that love lavished on me into strength and patience for the grandchildren they never saw. I was not able to give any of it back in grown-up companionship. Now my children are going through what I went through then. Dear God—let my parents' gifts help me to be more helpful. Not to be hurt by what seems to be rejection; I *know* it is a struggle for life.

Back home on the dresser I have a picture of my mother and father on their wedding day. On the desk is another taken outside our house when they had been married some twenty years. I remember when I used to think of both, then only of the second, as being of people much older than I. Now we are almost the same age. How I wish they were here so I could tell them I feel close to them, so we might enjoy things together. As I go to Gate 15, mingled in the confusion of passengers and loudspoken announcements, I think I hear their voices.

****

I am getting high listening to Dietrich Fisher-Dieskau pour *lieder* at me through the stereo speakers of the car radio. I'm waiting for my youngest to be deposited on this corner by the school bus so I can take him to an appointment. The trees are bare now and the soft purple hills just visible (through the windshield) behind their dark tracery. The music blends with trees and hills; it seems almost to speak for them—spacing, silence, duration and change. It strikes the chord of this bit of creation and sets it humming.

When I was young I would not have felt free enough in such a public place to notice how the sound and time of the music expressed the matter around me. I would have been worried about what that passerby might think of one playing music so loudly in the car.

An ad says, "TIME makes everything more interesting." It's true about the music; it's true about me. It's *not* true about *time*. That's distracting, dispersing. Just what the *lieder* are not. They focus, vitalize, intensify. To me they recall the insight into reality of the anonymous medieval lyric speaking in Christ's voice:

> Tomorrow shall be my dancing day
> I would my true love did so chance
> To see the legend of my play
> To call my true love to my dance.

> *Sing oh! my love, oh! my love, my love, my love,*
> *This have I done for my true love.*

Then, after he relates his whole life and death in the intervening stanzas, he concludes:

> Then up to Heaven I did ascend
> Where now I dwell in sure substance
> On the right hand of God, that man
> May come unto the general dance.

Life *is* a cosmic dance. The poem's timing is so true, it transcends time.

Here comes my son!

****

In New Orleans for a week-long meeting, I managed nevertheless to have my first Jungian dream. At least it seemed so to me. I had been outdoors in the dream, in a sunny green woods, when enormous multicolored butterflies drifted by. I looked down at the earth and saw that deep in holes beneath rabbits were thrusting themselves upwards, not just emerging, but throwing themselves into birth. In some fear I managed to kill a threatening snake, then wondered joyously at the creation around me.

Just the day before, I mused in that slow interval of realization after waking, I had told the group whose discussions I was chairing that Cunneen means "little rabbit" in Gaelic. A month or so before I had read Jung's *Memories, Dreams and Reflections*; he had frequently dreamed in terms of profound symbols that revealed his developing character and career to himself. I had marveled at the nature of his dreams, for mine—frequent enough—have been almost wholly related to people and incidents I know or have known, old houses, forgetting my part in a play, replays of the day's problems. As I lay in bed I realized that this dream, which had seemed like an illumination of matter from within, compelling affirmation, was related to the preceding day's events in more than name only.

I remembered that in the course of what had been an impossible series of responsibilities, challenges, encounters and reports, I had suddenly recalled the words spoken to me by a friend almost a year earlier. We had been looking at Chinese sculpture in the Metropolitan Museum. She herself sculpts after concentrated intellectual work, and I had asked her how it felt. Smiling strangely she said, "I just trust my unconscious."

Walking between the hotel and the convention hall on Canal street, I vainly tried to prepare to meet the five panelists who did not know each other or exactly what they were to speak about. Yet the group awaiting us hoped to gain something important by attending. Local groups had sent them to bring back information and techniques to the parishes back home. The meetings had been arranged for participation and feedback, yet the rigid, attached rows of chairs and the raised dais made this difficult. Designed to improve our spiritual life, the program did not include prayer on its first day—an oversight of which I was reminded by a disappointed participant from the floor. Confronted by a shifting crowd of men and women all day long, we were nevertheless to come up with agreements at the end of the week to be presented to the total assembly.

Impossible! So sneak off for a Creole feast at the Court-yard of the Three Sisters? Be slightly condescending to the housewives and pastors from Kansas and Iowa whom you liked but whose opinions seemed so different from your own on political and theological issues that you despaired of reaching them? Or . . . why not trust your *unconscious?* The words hit me as surely as the damp morning air on the way to the Rivergate. Surely they could apply to dealings with people as well as with stone. As I entered the crowded hall I gave myself firm instructions: "Relax; you'll know what to do if you don't react too quickly, talk too soon. There is more to you than what you control."

So I spoke and listened—asked a volunteer to pray—un-clenched my mind and stomach and became almost calm in the midst of chaos. I have always had to prepare talks, write them, in order to say what I really want. Otherwise the sense of the crowd, the moment, tended to make my mind go blank. But that day I was able to give coherent talks without preparation. Practice, of course, helped. But I believe my self-programming was more responsible. I was able to *live* in what was going on, and when the time came to tell others about it, better able to summon resources of judgment and selection almost automatically for a group that wanted to hear about it. It's a good deal like acting. You get a palpable sense of how the audience feels. Yet you write the script and create the plot while you're performing. When the performance itself is in participation with a group that cares deeply whether or not the church becomes more responsive to people, whether old rituals can be rekindled to new life, whether women, or brothers, or children or bishops can find common ground to share their talents and their differences, the process is exhilarating. It is not prayer, yet it is preparation for it in the community. I am reminded of the sage advice of Archbishop Bloom, who cautions those who believe they wish to pray not to demand too much of God's presence. That is always an act of mercy, and most of the time we are not prepared for it. Better to ask him to prepare us in what ways are needed to be ready when he comes.

Our preparation as a community was instructive to me. When a woman jumped up after the morning's discussion on the need for greater communication between clergy and laity and said, "What we need is for our priests to be more perfect Christians, models for the rest of us," I did not panic at what seemed the distance between us. It is amazing how tensions and antagonisms can erupt in a group and yet later, through what seems a living process, balance extreme personal claims and yet preserve tender feelings. Truth, love and hope can develop in the dynamics of a group that cares about the purpose of its meeting. Divisions tend to make responses more intensely honest, as long as a *translation* process occurs.

For translation, too, is part of preparing the community for prayer. Not jumping too soon to conclusions about others' opinions helped me to find out about the alcoholic background of the woman who counseled perfection to priests. I learned that much suffering and discipline had gone into her apparently simplistic assertion. While I could scarcely agree with her opinion that reform in the church should begin by removing the wine from the mass, it was amazing how much we could agree on. The differences were of style and emphasis. Parting, I found that she could keep her viewpoint yet I need not suppress mine.

Having tried it once, I was prepared for more during the afternoon panel on the changing role of women in church and society. After the sisters and lay women from around the globe (including an observer at the Vatican Council) had spoken in many voices of the same need for women to assume more public responsibility today, a woman arose and said: "I don't see why we have to worry about women's rights. We should just be obedient to the voice of the spirit within us. The aim is to be totally unselfish."

I feared that perhaps, if this response was possible after the reasoned explanations from the panel, we might be in for fruitless crossfire. "Yes," I replied nevertheless, counting on the power of unconscious translation, "you're absolutely right. That's the aim for all of us, it's true. But (the unconscious had begun to whir) you have to have a self to give, of course. Some women unfortunately take on patterns cut by others and never realize the self that can open up within them so they can hear the spirit in the way you speak."

"*You're* absolutely *right!*" she agreed. "You need a strong sense of identity and that's just what many women lack!" People are so surprising. At first contradiction and ominous hints of battle. But try another tack, use another lingo till you hit the rich vein of common experience and you may be enriched by unexpected wisdom. Our meeting came alive with people talking to each other across boundaries of habit, age, sex and state in life. Trusting the unconscious was becoming more than a spectator sport.

It was for me, I decided, as I rose from my dream-analysis to prepare for the next day's meetings. I had determined that my dream was a reward for trying what I should have been doing long before. It had reminded me powerfully of my scattered impressions on the intimate connections between physical and mental awareness. If I waken suddenly, as I did weeks after New Orleans, through a combination of a headache and the naked brightness of the full moon in my eye, I become aware of the strange process in which some late-night thought or experience works itself into my arms, shoulders, some material part of me. Seeing the moon that night and becoming aware of this indescribable yet frequent process, I remembered my dream again. The moment gave me an extraordinary sense of God's presence in creation—in and through *everything*—a hint of what Francis saw in Brother Wolf, Sister Moon. I was blessed (through the headache? my inadequacy to run the meeting?) with a glimpse of the splendor of creation entirely different from what I see with my waking eye.

Perhaps the most intriguing insight left me by these experiences is the feeling that when one trusts the unconscious, it is possible to love . . . everyone. Not fighting to overcome instinct, not giving things up, disciplining oneself, but letting go in the midst of life. Being able to do things better by not being so prepared as to be unprepared for the surprises that lie at the heart of creation. Even, by having no time, to find time.

Such experiences do not disappear and disappoint. They bring past and present together in a new focus. This one was for me like the opening of a new wing in the house of awareness that is now available for everyday use. It accommodates long-dead exotic aunts who sang for you and new young unexpected friends, but it never seems strange or big. You feel at home. This is the kind of preparation Archbishop Bloom referred to, I believe, as preparation for the mercy of God's revelations. It is instructive to note that he advocated humility as the only possible attitude to encourage this preparation we need in order to endure the light.

True humility, this wise monk reminds us, is closely related to the meaning of the Latin root *humus*, fertile ground. It is the situation of the earth, he tells us:

> The earth is always there, always taken for granted, never remembered, always trodden on by everyone, somewhere we cast and pour out all the refuse, all we don't need. It's there, silent and accepting everything and in a miraculous way making out of all the refuse new richness in spite of corruption, transforming corruption itself into a power of life and a new possibility of creativeness, open to the sunshine, open to the rain, ready to receive any seed we sow and capable of bringing thirtyfold, sixtyfold, a hundredfold out of every seed. (*Beginning to Pray*, 1970, Paulist Press, p. 11.)

Not putting up too much conscious resistance to the deep silent workings of my own unconscious was somewhat similar. It allowed for some preparation of the self. Even that was a sharp reminder of how unprepared I am, no matter how I thirst. Frankly, I couldn't have taken any more enlightenment, just now. The best I can do is ask for more preparation, in hope of being ready for the surprise of a merciful visit, but I ask for it piecemeal—slowly.

FAITH BELONGS
ON MAIN STREET

Since late 1972, DOUGLAS ROCHE has been a freshman Member of the Canadian Parliament (Conservative Party). A veteran newspaper and magazine writer, he is former editor of the successful weekly Western Catholic Reporter, *Edmonton, Alberta, and of* Sign *magazine. With his wife and five children, he resides—when not in Ottawa during sessions of the House of Commons —in Edmonton, Canada.*

by Douglas Roche

THE BELL IN THE PEACE TOWER IS CHIMING. I LOVE THE DEEP resonance of the sound, the sturdiness of it, the security that when it strikes the hour, there is no room for doubt. I stand at my office window in the Parliament Buildings, a back-corridor office, as befits a new Member of Parliament, looking to the rear instead of on the broad expanse of lawns in front. The dome of the Parliamentary Library is just ahead and I can almost touch it. Then the bluff and down below the Ottawa River, separating the cities of Ottawa and Hull.

I can see a church steeple over on the Hull side and its bell is also pealing, for this is the noon hour. A terrible roar echoes through the scene as the daily firing of the cannon marks the midday. Then the final notes of the Peace Tower Clock and the last tingling sounds of the church bell. Silence. A moment to think about the two bells, their difference for modern society, their difference in my own life.

But another bell, the phone, interrupts the reflection. The call leads to another, a luncheon guest has arrived, my question for the two o'clock Question Period in the House has to be prepared, committee meetings are ahead for the remainder of the afternoon and evening. A vote is scheduled

51

for 9:45 P.M. I know, without thinking about it, that it will be 10:40 exactly when I get up from dictating correspondence and head for my apartment.

Ritualistically (I like being on time for everything I do, there's something of the monk in me), I will walk into the apartment at 10:55, just in time to change into my pajamas, get a 7-Up and two donuts from the fridge, pick up two daily newspapers and settle down before the 11 o'clock TV news. There are books and magazine articles stacked beside my bed, but chances are I'll fall asleep reading before midnight.

The alarm will go off at 7:00 A.M. The daily routine will start. On the run. There won't be enough time to do the constituency and Parliamentary work already on the desk. My secretary will bring in a fresh load, right on schedule. I'll be irritable—I usually get over it—because there won't be enough time to read and study even the minimum necessary to stay abreast. Always the clock. The daily schedule of commitments. When will there be time to develop and legislate the sides that have brought me this far? Time. The most precious commodity a politician has.

Always the clock. The Peace Tower, chiming again. That sound, reassuring, steadies me. I used to lie in bed at night when I was a boy and listen to it. That was thirty years ago and we lived about a mile from Parliament Hill. Sandy Hill was a nice, convenient place to live, but now the modest house I grew up in has been torn down to make way for the expanding University of Ottawa. It gives me a strange feeling to see my sophomore daughter dashing into the University library that now dominates "my street." It was a peaceful, shady street. I remember bread and milk and ice being delivered by horse-drawn carts. We never seemed to mind the mess the horses made on the street. We just took life for granted—of course, that's the boy speaking. My parents must have worried about the bills in those depression years, but they never revealed their worries—at least not in front of the children.

Around the corner was the church, two huge churches, if you can believe, both Catholic. One for the English-speaking, the other for the French. United in faith, divided in culture. Separate but equal, something like that. Anyway, St. Joseph's was our church and it was like a second home for me (it wasn't that I prayed that much, there were parish tennis courts beside the church and socials in the parish hall).

A Catholic ghetto is what we would call it now—except that it was a very pleasant ghetto. It was our world. From serving the 6:30 A.M. mass, to the sodality meetings, to the companionship with the priests (there were always lots of priests around). Daily mass was more or less routine, Sunday evening benediction the custom (I was always proud that I could sing *Tantum Ergo* in Latin even though I didn't know what it meant) and Saturday afternoon confession mandatory, according to my mother's rules. If all this could be called infused spirituality, I was infused.

The years passed, missions, the Forty Hours, the candle-light procession at Midnight mass on Christmas Eve, the visits of Father (usually with a visiting Father) to the house. Catholic faith and Catholic culture. The two were so inter-twined, they were one. Of course, Jack Benny and Fred Allen and Fibber McGee were welcomed into our house on the new radio, but they were just diversions. The media then was clearly not the message. Our minds were formed by the Catholic church, the Catholic school, Catholic culture and Catholic friendships. I can remember when some distant relative was divorced; the couple might just as well have dropped off the face of the earth. And sex. Definitely taboo in household talk.

Narrow? Confining? I don't ever recall thinking that. I never wanted to rebel against a restrictive upbringing. I had a lot of fun. That is the way life was. I did want to break loose for a summer and go to Europe when I was nineteen, but that was mainly so I could see Rome and the Pope. I guess most people assumed I would be a priest. It was only when I was trying out a novitiate that the excessive cultural conformity of the clerical church got to me. Either it was too regimented, or I was not disciplined enough. But suddenly I began to feel my horizons too close to me. It was the first stage of a new spiritual perception. The Catholic faith-Catholic culture bond still entwined me, but it was loosening as I struggled for more room to maneuver.

I went to work writing obits for the local newspaper (my official biography describes this period as the beginning of my journalism career). I went back to college and That Girl became a preoccupation. We went to church together. Dances, too. Great college years. I founded a yearbook, announced a contest for the best title, named it "The Best Years" and gave myself the prize. Graduation, into the newspaper business. When the time came to be engaged, we went back to the college chapel to slip on the rings.

Marriage, babies, bills, job changes, the familiar pattern. I felt an attraction to the Catholic press because it seemed to me that this was journalism with a meaning. My roots in Catholic culture were so strong that I looked on it as fortuitous that I could combine my faith with a way to earn my living. I was a formal Catholic, an institutional Catholic. The church had the answers; my questions had not yet become very tough. Butler's *Lives of the Saints* fascinated me and it seemed natural to say the rosary in a family setting. Prayer, to me, was still formalized. If you prayed hard enough, your prayers would be answered. Lose something? St. Anthony. In a hopeless situation? St. Jude. Trying to be a good husband and father? St. Joseph. Answers, security, salvation. The Catholic church was home, wherever you were.

And then came the '60s. Bittersweet years in which I finally broke out of Catholic culture and grasped the meaning of my faith in deeper terms. My life shifted into a larger arena and, perhaps strangely for a "cradle Catholic," it was here that I discovered Christianity.

Obviously, this was not a one-man effort. The whole world was in upheaval and every old value seemed to come under attack. Pius XII was gone and John XXIII had opened the window. John F. Kennedy's sophisticated secularism proved, finally, that Catholics can find their way to center stage. The technological revolution, the cultural upheaval, religious experimentation; little by little, book by book, person by person, I was reaching out. Not too far, though. I still thought, in the early stages, that the Vatican Council would project the old answers in a modern idiom. Schillebeeckx and Küng were still to get through to me that answers would elude us until we had the courage to face the real questions of the church in the world.

I was lucky in the '60s because I traveled a lot and kept making personal discoveries. It was a shock to walk through the church of the Holy Sepulcher in Jerusalem, built on the very spot where Christ died that all may be one in him, and see the denominational squabbling over rights to the church. I spent a morning walking through the Garden of Gethsemani all by myself. It was there that the ridiculous tragedy of Christian division hit me full in the face.

I went to Africa and India, and the Third World opened up to me. A world of much suffering and culture and pride. I made the amazing discovery that the white, Western world is by no means superior in the family of man. For a moment, I could see from an African and Asian viewpoint how Western technology has dehumanized man.

The identification of the church with the West (the Medieval West) distressed me. In Bombay, I was amazed to see Catholics in church dressed as Westerners instead of the clothing of their fellow Indians. In the jungles of Africa, I couldn't figure out why hymns were being sung in Latin. Western missionaries had brought the teaching and love of Christ with them to foreign lands, but I became convinced that it was the failure of the church to adapt itself to the culture of the people in every part of the world that retarded the influence of Christianity in the Third World.

I went to Latin America, too, and here I saw, in human terms, the effect of the traditional alignment of the church with the established social classes. I spent some time studying the life of a Venezuelan Communist leader who had left the church because he was convinced the church would not involve itself in the struggle for social justice. When he was thrown in jail the first time for labor agitation, he recalled, it was a Communist leader, not a priest, who came to him. The poverty of the millions living in hillside shacks was overwhelming and the contrast of this inhumanity with the colossal church buildings and finely-appointed residences for Vatican nuncios unbelievable. I began to understand the dilemma of advanced Christian leaders whether to support revolution or work for social change through existing institutions.

I remember the very astute young lady who was our tour guide in Moscow. She willingly took us to the old churches of the Kremlin, for she was proud of the architecture, superlative paintings and cultural inheritance that had come down through the years. But the churches were for her just museums—buildings that people gawked at to see history. "Religion is history," she said and, in response to the challenge of our group, insisted that when the social and political revolution came to Russia, the church was nowhere to be found. "We built our new society without God," she said.

I also had an education in racism and this, too, affected my spiritual outlook. In the early '60s protests and demonstrations were still on the passive side. One day in Oklahoma City, I went to some downtown restaurants with a Negro lady and her teen-age daughter. We were turned away at the doors of all but one because there was "no room." In one place, we slipped in quickly and sat down—only to be ignored for 45 minutes during which we were the object of hateful stares. The woman I was with told me her grandmother was illiterate, her mother had gone as far as Grade 8, she herself had a Master's degree and her daughter intended to become a psychiatrist. I could only sit there quietly and be ashamed of my white skin.

These experiences gave me a perspective of the church I had never had before. The dichotomy between its inherent universality and the overlay of Roman protectionism made me critical, as I had never been before. I saw that we had fractured Christ, imposed our cultural standards on a supposedly pagan people, played a weak role in the struggle of people everywhere for social justice, and determined the quality of our faith by institutional survival and personal sanctification. I was in a mood for Vatican II.

In Rome during those years, a new understanding of the faith came into focus for me. I could almost feel the vibrancy of the Constitution on the Church and the Constitution on the Church in the Modern World. *Collegiality. Coresponsibility.* Marvelous words. *Continuing reformation. A pilgrim people. The desire to serve the world, not dominate it.* Euphoria.

And then anxiety. It wasn't working, or at least it didn't seem to be working. Backlash. Fallout. Chaos. What to pray to or for? I was editing a Catholic newspaper in the postconciliar years and thus felt early in the new era that the new form of the church, whatever it would be, was still over the horizon, probably the horizon of my life. I wrote a book, *The Catholic Revolution,* on the turmoil and reform in which I tried to explore the creativity that was a truer historical index than the sensational headlines of confrontation. I was beginning to take refuge, for the sake of my own mental balance, in some words Cardinal Leger spoke to me before he left for Africa: We have become so used to instant everything in the technological age that we think we can have instant reform in the church just because we had a Council. The human being is far more complex than a piece of machinery, the Cardinal reflected, and we've got to get over the idea we can produce postconciliar Catholics on an assembly line.

A paragraph at the conclusion of my book now seems, on re-reading a few years later, to have been prophetic about my own continued development, which was already a considerable distance from the sanctuary of Sandy Hill. I described the forthrightness that prompted many Catholics to search for a postconciliar spirituality that could be integrated into their human existence. "These Catholics no longer look to spiritual 'exercises' to keep fit. What they desire is a faith that helps them to see that life itself is a religious practice, to achieve a way of existence that ends the dichotomy between religion and life. Faith then ceases to be a comfort. It is a constant challenge, raising haunting questions about the human condition around us, the poverty, the racial discriminations, the underdeveloped countries. Catholics at this level are less concerned with the 'churchy' qualities of renewal and are eager for the church to end all the institutional trivia that prevents it from being a powerful conscience and critic of the social ills in the world."

"Life itself is a religious practice." This phrase seems to have sunk deep inside me as we try to cope with the fantastic contradictions of life in the '70s when the credibility of all institutions is so low. If I was already in a process of escaping the bounds of my Catholic culture in order to discover the universal meaning of the faith, the Vatican Council was certainly the instrument that codified the process. The deeper into the Council I plunged mentally, the more I could see that faith belonged on Main Street. Not the evangelical, street-corner witness-faith (at least for me). But an identification with the social process in the community and hence a chance to participate in the input into the value system.

Elementary? Perhaps for some. But for me it had to be a long journey to be able to live with the insecurity of not having all the answers. The process made me more conscious of the base I stand on and as I scratched away the accouterments around me, I found the pristine Gospel and saw in a new light the Sermon on the Mount. Again, it was Vatican II thinking that new forms could not be legislated but would have to emerge from within us and that—speaking for myself—I would have to look inside me rather than at the Vatican or my parish church, to find out what kind of church was possible. I have lost the surety I had when the Council came to its more glorious end in 1965 but in the interval have acquired more confidence in myself and my recognition of the spirituality of daily existence.

I know that many people are asking: What is the new form of prayer in this destructured institution? I have not made any conscious attempt to find a new form. And I do not think it is good to take a predetermined stance on prayer form if we are to grow in our appreciation of the sacredness of the world. In this, I have been influenced and helped by the writings of Michel Quoist (spiritual reading, very selective, is still part of my input). I find Quoist offering an integral view of the spirituality of the world, a joy in the fullness of God's creation. His prayers for various situations, the pedantic and spectacular, are a stimulus. He has a good antidote for the "vacuum" so many feel when formally praying. Too many of us rely on the "transcendence idea" of praying to the Father; rather, we should give ourselves to the absorption of Christianity, commit ourselves to the great advantage of creation, incarnation, redemption, resurrection, the fullness of God's plan. Work for the real development of man, mankind, the universe. "To be thus committed is to commit one's life to and with the people who live around us, in our natural societies, in our social

milieux, in our groups, structures, events and history. It is
to become inwardly involved, so that we may live the total
reality of life and of what lies beyond life."

Well then, what do you do with this new perspective,
this central idea? Preach it? Pray it? Meditate on it? For me,
absorbing it is (in the vernacular of my children) "where
I'm at." In reaching out, I'm happier within. Security is
elusive. I'm trying to live with it.

Not for a moment do I doubt that Christianity is enriched by the demythologizing we have gone through in the
past decade. I found myself being invited to speak at a lot of
Protestant and Anglican churches in my community. I told
my listeners frankly how important Christian reconciliation
was for me; and the response I received was consistently
warmer than I felt with Catholic audiences. Deep friendships blossomed from these inter-Christian contacts. When
the time came to make a decision whether to run for Parliament, it seemed natural for me to gather together fifteen
ministers of various denominations to get their reactions
and advice to my thinking about political involvement. "I
hope you don't get swallowed up by that big governmental
machine in Ottawa," one of my Baptist friends commented.
What he meant was that he hoped my basic motivation as a
Christian in politics would not be trampled in the political
process.

I don't want to give the idea that I entered the political
arena with a savior complex. I am not under the illusion
that one man alone can turn society around, but it was
Vatican II that cleared my head, or gave me the impetus,
or what have you to become involved in the governmental
process and to bring to it a value system that traces itself

back to the Gospel. There are other elected politicians who feel as I do, so I don't want to pretend that I'm breaking ground alone. (One of my colleagues in Parliament, an Anglican priest, upon being asked by a reporter if he would go back to the ministry if he were defeated, replied, "I have never left it.")

But it is a simple fact that too many decisions are made in government and Parliament for sheer (if not crass) political reasons and there is a strong need to reinforce human values at this moment in our history. The unemployment crisis, the housing shortage, the income security system are profound moral subjects. What is a better prayer: to go to a liturgical service to pray for peace and justice or to go to a committee meeting to put one more brick in place (if it's been a good meeting) in building a better society? Perhaps it doesn't have to be either/or. But for me the action-center has changed and that fact (God help me) constitutes a new prayer form.

The days ahead will call for calmness, determination and expert knowledge because the questions of life and death will be in our hands. Abortion, euthanasia, capital punishment are all coming before us in Parliament and there are those whose resolution of the conflict between pragmatics and the right to life is not the same as mine, to put it mildly. If I am to influence my colleagues on these high level issues, the spiritual issues, I have to have their respect in the workmanship of day-to-day drudgery of the unspectacular.

I hope the Lord understands when I dash off in the mornings without much contemplation of his goodness. I still like contemplation; the problem is that it doesn't get a high enough priority on the schedule. I think that's my fault, but so be it. I would still like to go off to a monastery for a few days of peace and meditation and reading—but now I feel guilty about taking the time from my family because my political life already short-changes them.

Pressures all around me. The prime years, so they say. The church no longer an umbrella. My children struggling through their own crises of what to believe in. The life and love of Jesus is a steadying influence and each one, I think, must find it for himself. With help, of course. We find help in strange places. Like the Peace Tower clock outside my window. When I hear its powerful bell toll the hours, I hear the sounds of courage and patience.

AGONIZING BUT
NOT IN DESPAIR

*ALBERT MILLER is an Assistant
Professor of Political Science at Chicago's Mundelein College. A Fulbright Scholar and a Danforth Fellow, Mr. Miller has published several
articles on the subject of black/white
student relations. He was formerly on
the staff of* The Critic. *He recently
returned, with his wife and children,
from sabbatical studies in Africa.*

by Albert Miller

A RETREAT, A NOVENA, A DAY OF RECOLLECTION, A PARTICULAR time of day or week and place for solitary prayer and frequent short meditations. For more than 40 years these have been external expressions of my spiritual life. Today, I cannot recall being engaged in even one of these traditional activities during the last five years. I grew up believing that together with the mass these forms of prayer and meditations and reflections were normal healthful forms of spiritual life. And if, except for attending mass, I do not practice any of them today, it is not because one day I suddenly decided that these practices were no longer beneficial or that the idea of a "spiritual life" had become anachronistic.

Nor does my lack of practice of the traditional forms of Roman Catholic spirituality have anything to do with religious "modernism" or the present spread of Roman Catholic "Pentecostalism" or the "rat race" of present-day life. I don't know exactly how it came about that novenas, days of recollection, retreats, various other devotions, etc. gradually ceased to have personal spiritual value for me. Though I will risk speculating that my loss of interest in these spiritual forms probably occurred in a manner analogous to the way one honestly loses faith. Gradually or suddenly the once faithful becomes conscious of the fact that he no longer believes one or more "articles of faith." Likewise I slowly became conscious of the fact that traditional forms of "spiritual life," including private prayer, no longer fulfilled any experienced need in my life. No matter how it occured, over how long a period of time or how complicated the psychological process involved, it happened that I slowly became conscious of the meaninglessness of these traditional spiritual practices in my life. I stopped the practices accordingly.

As it was occurring it was not altogether clear to me why the traditional forms of spirituality no longer appeared meaningful to me. Had it been all that clear I suspect I would have had some idea of what alternatives, if any, would have been more satisfying to me. But I didn't, although later I will suggest some reasons why I think novenas, retreats, days of recollection and even audible forms of private prayer no longer seem spiritually meaningful to me.

Yet since I no longer practice traditional forms of spirituality the question at the moment is whether there is any sense in which I consider that I have any spiritual life at all. My answer to that question is an emphatic yes. However, in spite of the emphasis the statement doesn't say very much because I believe everyone, believer and nonbeliever, has some kind of spiritual life. I am still a believer, so what is required of me is that I describe those characteristics of my life that constitute my spiritual life even though the forms and practices have no recognized relationship to traditional forms of spirituality. This is difficult for me to describe, because I am not sure that everything I am going to call a sign of my spiritual life is unambiguously so. But that is a risk accompanying any attempt to describe significant change in anyone's life.

The problem here is one of not always knowing for certain what it is I actually do that I experience as spiritually satisfying as the older forms of activities which I have very nearly abandoned.

Today the only traditional religious activity that I regularly participate in is the mass. I go to mass in spite of the fact that most times I don't "get out of it" the spiritual satisfaction I once did. Still, I continue to attend. But I don't do so out of fear of violating any canonical regulation or out of any sense of guilt if I don't do so. In fact both during and immediately after mass I more often undergo a state of mild depression rather than one of spiritual uplifting. This feeling is not associated with any psychological process that I understand theologians associate with a loss or a losing of faith. Rather, my depression is associated with the feeling that neither I nor most of my coworshipers actually experience a common sense of relationship (and thus fulfillment) between the liturgical action and the spiritual reality and need of our day-to-day lives. In the absence of the experience of such a meaningful relationship the liturgy fluctuates between appearing boring and bizarre and I and my fellow worshipers appearing strange and silly. There is that lack of a sense of community at the very heart of liturgical community.

Given this sense, this feeling of the emptiness of the mass, why do I continue regularly to attend? Part of the answer to that question is the simple, honest one that I do it out of habit. The more conscious and deliberate reason why I attend mass—even though I anticipate it is going to be empty and boring—is because I feel the need for a public, liturgical expression of that centrality of spirituality and meaning of that profound sense of community, of a relationship to God and my fellow man, in my life that I used to experience in the mass. No other form of private or public worship provides that spiritual need in my life today. So I continue going to mass out of habit and hope.

If I have slowly abandoned other traditional religious practices and find the mass itself often an unsatisfying experience, is there any form of activity that expresses a life of the spirit for me? Yes—but. In addition to the mass, there are some things I do that sometimes are at least as spiritually meaningful to me (and sometimes they are more meaningful) as any of the traditional forms of prayer life I regularly participated in. The difference is that this happens infrequently, irregularly, and is usually private. For example, I used to go to church, get down on my knees and say approved and "prescribed" prayers daily, these in addition to my own deliberate, spontaneous prayers. Now it has been so long ago that I don't know when was the last time I prayed while on my knees, either in church or at home. But it is not only that I do not pray while on my knees any more. I don't say traditionally prescribed or approved prayers at all, except at mass, and I have adopted no alternative bodily posture or prayers. But I still pray.

I can and do pray in all manner of positions and situations. Sitting at my desk, driving to work, watching a football game, listening to and talking with my wife and children, friends and strangers, lecturing my class, counseling a student. You name it. In all these situations and relationships I can and do praise God—a triune God at that—for his own unfathomable self. I thank and praise him for the goodness of his creation, especially his human creation—

for those human manifestations of love, helpfulness and honesty in a world in which these often appear to be vanishing virtues.

I say that for me there often are occasions and circumstances in which I actually pray. But just as these prayers are neither formula nor prescribed prayers neither are they audible or said while on my knees. They are spontaneous and silent and conform to no contemporary religious institutional teaching about how to pray, though I think my own prayer life is perfectly consistent with some of the instructions of some early spiritual writers. A famous theologian has said that the proper posture of man before God is "on his knees." But the prostration of men before men—nobles before kings, for example—who rose from their "posture" of deference and respect to cut off the crowned head in front of them raises questions as to how we are to interpret these pious offerings. Isn't it the position of the heart, the attitude of mind, the whole disposition of the person that these pious statements must refer to if they are to have any intelligent applicability across time and space?

As with private prayer in a nonprescribed, nonkneeling posture, today my experience is similar with regard to what we used to call devotional exercises, including spiritual reading, retreats, novenas, etc. As I have said, I have long since ceased to find any satisfaction in participating in those traditional forms of spirituality. Today, as I have also indicated, some things I find myself doing are sometimes even more satisfying than traditional devotions and sometimes less so.

But what I find least satisfying about my present "devotional" experiences is that the occasions when the experiences are spiritually satisfying are too infrequent; there is nothing as regular as an old-fashioned Friday night novena, and of course, most times these are private occasions. My problem with a spirituality that is altogether private is that it tends to form, to create little religious cliques, whereas the essence of the mass and some associated traditional devotions is the emphasis on the public character of the worship. The psychological and spiritual value of that emphasis for me is the sense of being related to my fellow man in a common action of understanding, love and worship. It is in great part because they usually lack a public character that no alternate devotional action today consistently has the spiritual meaning for me that the mass and devotions once did.

Take, for example, spiritual reading or the study day or weekend of yesteryear. These recommended and prescribed exercises used to be satisfying to me. They haven't satisfied me for a long time and I don't participate in them any more. The truth of the matter is that I find more spiritual inspiration in reading and re-reading the *Autobiography of Malcolm X*; John Hersey's great novel of Warsaw ghetto Jews' magnificent resistance to their monstrous Nazi oppressors; the life, writings and lectures of Father Daniel Berrigan, to name only a few of the more famous recent and contemporary names. To study, to ponder the meaning of the life of a Malcolm X, a Daniel Berrigan has more value for me today than an entire Catholic encyclopedia of the Lives of the Saints. The tale of the Warsaw Jews' incredible resistance to Nazism or the little publicized suffering and resistance of Black Africans to Portuguese, Rhodesian and South African domination are more spiritually meaningful to me than all the tales about the terrible measures the Roman empire used to crush the catacomb Christians.

I would not be misunderstood. It is not that I belittle the spiritual treasure in the Lives of the Saints or in the persecution of the early Christians. After all I once perused them reverently and frequently. And I consider my own early study of those lives to have been instrumental and beneficial influences in my present attitude and outlook. It is just that the pattern and structure of evil and oppression that Malcolm X and Daniel Berrigan or the Warsaw ghetto Jews and contemporary Black Africans fighting against all odds and virtually alone against the remnants of European domination are more experientially real to me than are those of the classic Lives of the Saints. And, canonization aside, I have absolutely no reason to believe these people are any less in God's favor or any less material and spiritual benefactors of mankind than those the church officially presents to us for imitation and inspiration. The inspiration and devotion then that once resulted from prescribed, recommended and organized spiritual reading for me now comes more from the example of the lives of my contemporaries. And this without prejudice to the retention of these older forms of spirituality by other Christians and without disparaging the perpetual value of the Lives of the Saints.

There is a whole range of responsibilities and relationships I am routinely involved in, sometimes daily, in which I experience a spiritual dimension that is often more satisfying than most of the traditional devotions I once regularly participated in. As forms of encounter and relationship with people they bear no relationship to traditional modes of nourishing one's spiritual life. In my own family, my wife and I have spent hours sharing with each other our mutual and sometimes painful inability to find spiritual satisfaction in many modes of traditional worship and devotional exercises. Until we began to have problems with traditional methods of worship and devotion we never did explore with each other the depths of our feelings, the day-to-day implications of our faith. This was mostly prescribed, and it so happened that what the church prescribed was not contradicted by our experience. However, as we ceased to find satisfying the relationship between the approved and required religious practices and the spiritual needs of our own lives, we began to talk with each other about the developing gulf. This sharing of our mutual agony about our inability to experience satisfying meaning in traditional worship and devotions was (and still is) itself a "spiritual exercise" for us. A spiritual exercise the value of which vastly exceeds the value we received from the spiritual practices that were the object of our concern. If you don't go to confession, devotions, retreats, days of recollection, study days, etc., why don't you? The point is that to honestly try to answer these questions has been a profound spiritual experience for us.

My own view is that while to wrestle with these kinds of questions does not necessarily increase one's spirituality or bring one nearer to God, nevertheless the person undergoing the experience does retain a conscious relationship with God while simultaneously increasing the prospects that this religion will be meaningful in terms of the realities of his life and that of his fellow man. Thus religion while being associated with our relation to God does not risk denying a sordid world of men and things and human situations. Religion does not risk becoming a fantasy. To my wife and myself this mutual sharing of common agonies for the reasons that we engage in such exploratory sharing is itself a "spiritual exercise" though, granted, it meets no traditional prescription of a spiritual exercise.

The situation is similar with regard to our children. Their earliest experiences were in Catholic schools. My wife and I participated in almost all activities of the parish. That is to say our own behavior was a reinforcement, we believed, of the spiritual training our children were acquiring at school. It slowly dawned on us in our observation and discussions with the children that their religious exercises and even some religious teachings were not experienced by them as having any real meaning in their young lives. The specific manner in which we tried to help our children is not particularly germane. The whole discussion is about my spirituality. It is only necessary to note that it seemed to my wife and me pointless to discuss religion with our children in the manner in which it was discussed with us when we were adolescents. If we were having our own problems with many aspects of traditional religious practices, it seemed all the more reasonable that they might also.

If children—or even adults, for that matter—can no longer find value in inherently changeable religious forms and practices, is everything lost? Indeed, is anything lost if, like their parents, they cease participating in them? Personally, I think it is the character of the lives lived by the parents in and out of the presence of their children that in the last analysis is the controlling influence, if anything is. Our actual lives (not exercises) will be on display to them in the love, understanding, concern that we have for them and their problems. The "family community" that is enhanced by an authentic spiritual life of our own can be, I believe, more rewarding for the young person than any effort to convince him of the value of traditional religious exercises that neither he nor we find rewarding. I am arguing that this adult effort to help the adolescent find spiritual meaning in his life outside of traditional religious forms can be a profound spiritual experience.

Besides my day-to-day relationship with my family, other experiences of a spiritual dimension outside traditional religious practices come to mind. I think of a student-faculty discussion in which a minority of students requested that a majority of students and faculty justify their support of a resolution substituting a "teach-in" for normal course offerings for the remainder of a term in support of American student protest against continued U.S. involvement in the war in Vietnam. My initial experience was the fact that the overwhelming majority of faculty and students submitted to the request of a tiny minority of students. More importantly, in the midst of the most intense feelings of both sides of the issue, the moral and intellectual values that were invoked, the sheer moral and intellectual force of the arguments, and above all the absolute respect of the overwhelming majority for the views of the minority, left me with a feeling of a "community" of genuine concern for, an interest in understanding, and a care for each other. The experience of that discussion was more valuable, more rewarding to me than all of the courses I had taught and all the discussions I had engaged in during the entire year.

You will ask, what is spiritual about that little event involving a group of students and teachers? I answer that the spirit moveth and showeth where and to whom he will. The event is intended to point out that this is just one example of a spiritual experience for me that occurs during the course of my performing my ordinary daily responsibilities and that had more spiritual meaning than any traditional activities at the time I ceased participating in them.

Other experiences include the visit, while traveling, of a young priest to my home during the height of violent protests and the assassinations of Kennedy and King during the late 1960s. Much of our discussion was devoted to a consideration of violence and death—society's very narrow definition of violence and the possibility that venerated institutional structures and procedures may themselves be forms of violence more destructive of human rights and dignity than all of the physical violence of the decade. We talked about death and resurrection and how much we avoid any talk about death, perhaps because among other reasons we so little realize the profound sense in which our death is our life—the virtual certainty that what we live for is identical with what we would die for. The conversation was neither mystical nor lyrical, but most spiritually, morally and intellectually rewarding.

Another experience of a different genre would include a 15th wedding anniversary of a married couple. A simple home celebration with friends and relatives of a loving relationship through good times and bad times, ups and downs, failures and triumphs. Nothing spectacular, and certainly not traditionally liturgical, but for all that a moving experience of mutual love, concern, responsibility, community. More examples come to mind, but these should suffice to illustrate the point that the nourishment of my spiritual life, such as it is, comes more from my day-to-day encounters and relationships than through any traditional practices or exercises.

This discussion would be distorted, or at least not placed in proper perspective, if I did not mention that there are traditional forms of devotion and worship today that I sometimes participate in and, in the circumstances, often find as rewarding as I once did. But before I exemplify what any of these are it is important to mention that they are infrequent occasions and almost always involve someone I know as the principal reason for the occasion, and often many people I know as the participants. An example of this has been participation in some nun or priest friend's religious anniversary celebrations, some weddings and an occasional mass in which the worshipers seem as cold as a cemetery in the dead of winter. But then the celebrant, humbly yet consistently, prayerfully yet forcefully confronts the worshipers in a homily with a spirit and power that only the already spiritually dead would not be vivified by. He takes no party-line position. But he does say that the Good News came into the world among men under a set of social circumstances. It is not possible to ignore that fact if our religion is to make us truly human rather than to provide us with a split personality.

All this leads me to admit that it may be that the activities I have been suggesting as alternatives to traditional forms of spirituality in reality may not be alternative modes of "spiritual" activity at all. It may be that what I have been describing is nothing more than the incorporation into my routine day-to-day activities the substance of what we used to think of as the spiritual value of a set of activities separate from our routine day-to-day activities. If so, this incorporation would lend itself to at least two rather easy interpretations. That traditional forms of spirituality have contributed to effecting a synthesis between my "spiritual exercises" and my routine daily life and that, to the extent that traditional forms are being abandoned, they are no longer capable of bringing about such a synthesis. I take it as unarguable that such a synthesis is desirable. I believe that this is in fact the case.

In other words, I have come to believe that the forms of Catholic worship that were the established and accepted order of worship, including the mass, of the last several generations increasingly will fail to evoke a positive response in succeeding generations. And I don't think that this has anything to do with any lack of faith by this generation by comparison with past ones. It seems to me that I and many contemporary Catholics find retreats, novenas, days of recollection, spiritual reading, etc., obsolete in both form and content. They are obsolete in form because they represent a style of "spiritual" activity that is increasingly radically at odds with the style, the form and the structure of the everyday life of all of us. As styles, structures, organizations (these are what forms are) of spiritual activity the traditional devotions must become increasingly powerless and bizarre, as they become anachronistic relative to the forms of life of man in the modern world. These forms of prayer, of devotions, developed in an age where they were more congruent with the modes of life of the times in which they originated. This amounts to saying that the style, the forms of spiritual life cannot be experienced as too much at variance with the styles, the forms of modern life if the religious forms are to be perceived and experienced as meaningful to the experiences and minimum requirements of man in his ordinary work-a-day world. It is my belief that traditional forms of spirituality increasingly fail to meet that minimum requirement.

I have also said that not only the forms but also the content of traditional spirituality is obsolete. The content is obsolete because what we actually say and do (the content) in our traditional spiritual exercises and devotions is, like the form (the style), selected and prescribed in accordance with the spiritual emphasis that coincided with an intellectual view of God, man and the world rooted in a bygone age.

Let's face it, our age does not experience the world as being created, let alone being created by an omnipotent God. We experience ourselves as creators—not co-creators. We don't experience man as being dependent on God. Those of us who lack the consciousness at the core of our minds at least know in the marrow of our bones that we have less control over our lives and destinies today than at any time in the past. We know that by accident or intention in one unknowable instant some idiot can by a simple action reduce virtually the entire planet to a charnel house of radioactive dust. True, people don't organize their daily lives on the basis of these constant and terrible realities, but that is not to say that it is not a part of their psychic structure and thus an influence, however unconscious, on the perception of God, man and the world. The point of all this is that the content, like the form, of our prayer or devotional or spiritual life must give way to a content that does not do violence to (is not contradicted by) our experience—that does not have us praying words and actions that strain our sense of any credible relationship between these words/actions and the way we experience the world. But that is exactly what has come to pass.

I don't pretend to know what the solution is, but I am convinced that a solution is not made more difficult by those of us who frankly admit that we don't practice the traditional spiritual activities anymore, who admit that we don't find alternatives fully satisfying, and who as a result agonize over this difference with fellow worshipers.

IN SEARCH
OF FULFILLMENT

A native of Minneapolis-St. Paul, and a graduate of the College of St. Catherine, PATRICIA MOHS is a former researcher for Time-Life Books. Ms. Mohs lives with her husband, an associate editor for Time, *and two children in New York City.*

by Patricia Mohs

TERESA OF AVILA HAS ALWAYS BEEN MY FAVORITE NEW
Testament saint, though not for the usual reasons. Her life
as an ascetic and mystic did hold an attraction for me during the brief period I contemplated becoming a nun. But
it is an apocryphal image of Teresa the reforming peregrine
that has held my imagination and helped to shape my
spiritual life: Teresa caught on a mud road in a rainstorm,
shaking her fist at God and railing, "If this is the way you
treat your friends, no wonder you have so few. . . ." I remember first hearing this story of Teresa during the sixth
grade preparation for Confirmation, when afternoons were
devoted to studying the lives of saints in the hope that we
might pick appropriate patrons. Years later, studying scriptures in my freshman year at the College of St. Catherine,
I had occasion to recall Teresa once again.

The reluctant prophets of the Old Testament, it became
apparent, had set the pattern for the God-man relationship
later attributed to St. Teresa. One may love God, fear him,
be reverential and worshipful, but the intimacy of a relationship in which anger (or at least disappointment) can
be expressed has been important to me personally and has

81

helped to sustain me in my filial relationship with God
and his church. Knowing that God's love for me is irre-
vocable and that mine for him is at least nonrefundable
has allowed me to take some liberties God might not appreciate but has come to expect from this mortal.

During my seventeen years in Catholic schools many
solicitous teachers and religious took me aside and, referring
to my three mentally retarded sisters, explained, "God only
sends heavy crosses to those he loves." Over the years I have
become convinced that God does indeed try those he loves
—some with tragedy and the rest of us with nickel and dime
mishaps. I have never pretended to understand the incredibly complex theological structure designed to explain grace
(for that matter, the parallel structure for sin boggles my
mind), but I believe that there does exist some supernatural form of support available to those presented with
Job-like misfortunes. It is in the small griefs of life, when
we must fall back upon our own resources, that I think
God's whimsicality becomes apparent.

I lived most of my first twenty-one years in a closely knit
family in St. Paul, Minnesota. Our neighbors were, for the
most part, Catholic educators with large families. Politically
and religiously liberal, ethnically third and fourth generation Irish and German, philosophically hopeful if not optimistic, the neighborhood was a mirror image of my family.
As my normal sister, brother and I grew up our institutionalized sisters were important in our lives, as they were
part of most of our family outings and family celebrations.
Our grandparents, cousins, uncles and aunts were frequent
guests in our home. Whether we were alone or with family
or friends, our dinner table was a forum for the discussion

of the ethical, political and religious questions of the fifties and sixties.

Life in such a homogenous environment was never dull (my grandfather and father used to get in such hot debates over then-Agriculture Secretary Benson that my Grandmother Murphy once simply chose to faint), but it did not exactly prepare me for my current life. Perhaps one of the great myths accepted by Americans is that we can be prepared for anything life has to offer. Certainly no human being was prepared for the upheavals of the 1960s (the war machine in Washington is excluded from that generalization). Despite Christian marriage courses, Cana conferences and idyllic family backgrounds, few people can actually be readied for marriage and parenthood. Very few are prepared for their own retirement and old age. And the last rites notwithstanding, I doubt that any but the most exceptional individual is really prepared for his own death. It is not surprising, then, that upon my graduation from college in 1969 I found my degree in history and political science next to worthless for gaining employment in Minneapolis-St. Paul.

Fortunately, I didn't have to. Like some *deus ex machina*, one of my father's former students (who later became my husband) happened to come to town one weekend in May. Being my father's good friend, he offered to check out job possibilities for me with Time Incorporated, where he worked as a writer. One month later, armed with my rather uneven education and employment experience (five years of selling "intimate apparel" part-time in a department store) I took up residence on the Upper West Side of Manhattan and began researching various volumes for Time-Life Books.

Manhattan brings out the latent hedonist in most people. My husband still relishes the memory of taking me to the Metropolitan Opera House for the Stuttgart Ballet soon after my arrival. "The Great Radical" (as he loves to remind me whenever I slip into the "radic-lib" posture that the late unlamented Spiro so enjoyed mocking), fresh from the McCarthy campaign in "the ice of Wisconsin" and on the streets of Chicago, studied the crystal chandelier that dominates the hall and murmured, "I could learn to live like this." Great music, wine, food and entertainment are all available with a minimum of effort. The only limit imposed is the amount of money one has to spend on hedonistic pursuits—unless, of course, one has a conscience.

Forming an individual response not only to the obvious challenges of New York's sweet life but to the many private challenges of the penultimate polyglot society has presented me with many serious spiritual questions. Determining a Christian attitude in uncharted territory has never been simple. As my roles have changed from working-woman to working-married-woman to mother-of-one and now, mother-of-two, I have repeatedly had to redefine my perceptions of what it means to be a Christian, of what is just, of which choice among many is the right one. The answers—and the questions—are relatively new to me. Much of what I learned in Minnesota sometimes seems to have little application in Manhattan.

Through my years in Catholic schools, I had been taught that the burden of the Christian was to be different. I had little realization then that this differentness entailed being a Roman Catholic during a recrudescence of a Know-Nothing-like anti-Catholicism (the anti-Semitism of the intellectual, as Richard Neuhaus once called it); making a life-long commitment to one man during a period when marriage is regarded with suspicion, ridicule or hostility; bearing children in a time when pregnancy and child-rearing are viewed as slightly obscene if not reactionary activities.

When I left Minnesota, birth control was still a significant question for some of my friends. When I landed in New York, the State Assembly had defeated a change in the penal code that would permit abortion on demand; the neofeminists were mounting their last campaign for what they claimed was control over their own bodies and the rejection of the "Catholic sponsored" law which required them to bear the children they might conceive. (During the abortion debate one point has, amazingly, escaped notice: Most of the restrictive laws prohibiting abortion were on the books long before Catholics enjoyed full civil rights, much less significant voice in the various states' legislatures.) I had, by 1969, long thought of myself as a rather liberated woman. Having personally encountered sex-based prejudice, I felt a certain sense of solidarity with the early aims of the women's movement: equal treatment before the law, equal opportunities in educational and career pursuits. I had rejected the sweeping edict of the Vatican prohibiting any method of birth control other than the so-called rhythm method, feeling that, in most circumstances, rhythm is more unnatural than many of the "artificial" methods of limiting the size of one's family. I did not reject, however, the basic principle that life is sacred. The same ideals that led me to oppose the war in Viet Nam placed me in opposition to the calls for abortion on demand.

As the debate raged between the hysterical "sisters" and the strident "Right to Lifers" I began to feel cut off from both groups. I came to see the women's movement as as great a subjugator of women as even the most misogynistic Pope. (What is it if not denigrating to suggest that women are so basically irrational and incapable of self-control that a pill or an application can be forgotten or diaphragm neglected in "moments" of passion?)

My real disappointment was reserved, however, for the church militant, collared and lay. Beginning, as many of the Right to Life people did, with the unsound premise that equated birth control and abortion, abortion and infanticide, the points in opposition to abortion and in favor of defending human dignity and life—positive points that needed making—were lost in wild exchange. The Catholic bishops, while mustering plenty of supporters and marchers in opposition to changes in the various states' abortion laws, remained silent during most of the agony of the war in Viet Nam, lending a certain credibility to the pro-abortion lobbies' charges that the Catholic church as a whole cared only that unwanted children be borne to term with little or no regard for the lives faced by those children and their mothers.

Five years have come and gone. The Right to Life lobby is scurrying about seeking a Constitutional Amendment that would reverse the Supreme Court ruling of 1973 which permits, effectively, abortion on demand. Some advocates of the proposed amendment claim that the Constitution of the United States should state, unequivocally, that human life, from conception to natural death, is sacred and inviolable—at least within the confines of the fifty states. The basic law of the land—a land that denies amnesty to those individuals who refused to fight the war in Viet Nam, that refuses money to the World Bank in a year when twenty-two million people face death from starvation, that can't find the money to ensure food, clothing, education, decent shelter and a sense of dignity for its citizens but can muster ninety-nine billion dollars for the Department of Defense —would then, indeed, be on record as the great respecter of Human Life and Dignity. The irony of it would be cause for laughter, if you could hold back your tears.

When my husband, Mayo, and I were first married, the absence of family from our daily lives seemed almost a blessing. We were able to work out our adjustments and our problems by ourselves. The well-meaning advice from parents that some couples complain about was sharply limited by the amount of money we could spend on long distance telephone calls. The friction sometimes associated with the term "in-laws" was impossible with a thousand miles separating the nearest of us—but as it turned out, the distance was less a blessing than a source of melancholy. We liked—no, loved—our "in-laws"; vacation time with them was a joy. And as our family has grown, the lack of close family nearby has become more poignant. We have a loyal and warm "New York family" of friends, but they do not fill the same roles as grandparents, aunts and uncles.

Before our children were born, Mayo and I would usually lumber off to our respective floors of the Time-Life Building, occasionally meet for lunch, join each other for dinner. I came to an early understanding of the demands—psychological, physical and spiritual—that are placed on the editors of "The Weekly Newsmagazine." Being fatigued and frustrated by the same system, I was able to fall in bed at night without resenting (too mightily, at least) that my husband had to stay on at the office until two, three or four o'clock in the morning. Knowing that Mayo is fulfilling himself through his work helps me to come to terms with the occasional bouts of loneliness that I experience. Knowing that he is in many instances giving needed currency to issues and ideas of real importance is of some solace—even when I have been craving the sound of an adult voice attached to a human form rather than to a television screen or a radio loudspeaker.

With the birth of our first child, Matthew, an event we had long hoped for and anticipated, I quit working at Time-Life Books in favor of becoming a full-time mother. Every couple needs certain adjustments when the first child comes home from the hospital, but I find that I am adjusting still. No longer able to take off for a concert or movie on a moment's notice—or even a trip to the grocery store—I find that it is easy for tedium to set in, and if not tedium, frustration. (My secret longing has been for the days when I was able to accomplish something without such a procession of daily obstacles: In the course of my preparing this essay, our son Matthew cut all but his first six teeth, had the flu for seven weeks—which he passed on to me in all its splendor, broke his toe and, finally, caught the German measles from one source or another.) You have to come to terms with your frustration, and even anger, with the child you love and have prayed for. There comes a point, whether during the fifth month of colic or the cutting of the second molar, when each parent has to recognize his or her own hostile feelings. Those are the times for pragmatic spiritual

methods: Taking a pillow into the bathroom and pummel-
ing it for a few minutes, having a good cry, finding a quiet
spot and screaming. Such activities can quite re-order one's
mind and spirit (and prevent one from becoming a child-,
wife- or husband-beater). Prayers and contemplation and
the dicta of Thomas a Kempis may help the unusual individual, but more often than not, at four o'clock in the
morning, I find myself emulating the apocryphal Teresa:
shaking my fist in the direction of heaven and asking, "How
many more teeth can this child get?"

Fortunately love, while not conquering all, makes life
more than bearable. In Jan Troell's fine movie, *The New
Land*, the central characters, Kristina and Karl Oskar
Nilsson, must learn to cope with life in the new territory
of Minnesota, far removed from family, friends and the
familiar things of Sweden (a situation easily recognized by
today's new migrants, the corporate families). At the first
opportunity, Kristina plants an apple sapling she had
brought with her in steerage from the old country. In attempting to build a stable family with a sense of roots and
continuity, and somehow to compensate our children for
their necessarily being stuck with a nuclear family, I have
come to feel as though I too, in a way, am planting just
such apple trees.

Partly for that reason, attending mass at our neighborhood parish has become much more important to us now
than it was before Matthew was born. It is a good parish,
probably one of very few in New York City in which we
could feel so much at home. It is feisty, politically brave in
fighting for its poor, sharply aware of the rich ethnic spread
of its parishioners. One of its generous aspects is that the

diversity of the neighborhood is expressed in both the church art and its liturgy, not ignored as it might be elsewhere; Christmas Midnight Mass is sung in Spanish, French and English. At home, though our son is not yet old enough to understand the spiritual significance of Advent wreaths, ashes, palms and Easter candles, we have begun to introduce him to these family-centered observances.

Classical sainthood is something more than I hope for (or probably want). At twenty-six I have come to realize that creating a home that is relatively at peace and happy and hopeful is the Christian witness I can best bear. Bringing some comfort and joy into the lives of others is as great a challenge as participating in demonstrations. I can only hope, when my life is finally judged, that I will have done more good than harm, that I will have brought some joy into the lives of my family and friends, that I will have taught my children to respect themselves and other people and to be a part of their times.

One of our best friends, part of our New York "family," passed on a quotation from C. G. Jung that perhaps sums up what I hope my husband and I will be able to convey to each other and to our children:

> Fulfill something you are able to fulfill, rather than run after what you will never achieve. Nobody is perfect. Remember the saying, "None is good but God alone." And nobody can be. It is an illusion. We can modestly strive to fulfill ourselves and to be as complete human beings as possible, and that will give us trouble enough.

So it does.

TO BRIDGE
THE IRRECONCILABLE

Professor of Philosophy at the University of Melbourne, Australia, MAX CHARLESWORTH has also lectured in England, Belgium, Italy, Japan and the United States. He was one of the founders of the Catholic Peace Movement in Australia and is now a co-editor of the monthly Catholic Worker. *Formerly a lay consultor to the Vatican Secretariat for Non-Believers, Mr. Charlesworth and his family live in Melbourne.*

by Max Charlesworth

BEING AGE 47 AND WELL PAST DANTE'S "MID-POINT OF LIFE'S way," my religious psyche was laid down at a time in the church when it was still possible to speak without embarrassment of the "interior life," "mental prayer," "contemplation" and all that, and when it was still acceptable for Catholics to write and read books with titles such as *The Story of a Soul, Journal of a Soul* and so on. According to the then prevailing view, the cultivation of the spiritual life required a withdrawal from the secular sphere and from the world of action. You retreated, in St. Augustine's words, "into the private cubicle of the soul" and there in that inner private sanctum you confronted God face to face. And this meant that you could not pray, or lead a religious life, "on the run"; rather, you had to stop running and take time out in order to nurture your soul.

I think that I now appreciate clearly enough the inadequacies and dangers of that way of talking and thinking about the religious life, based as it was upon a kind of Cartesian split between the private and the public or social self, and also upon a hard and fast distinction between "contemplation" and "action." But, at the same time, I am

93

also wary of some of the tendencies of post-Vatican II
theology which end up by identifying the religious life with
one's action in the world and with one's life of active
charity toward one's fellow men.

According to this post-Vatican II view, to fight for social
justice for the oppressed, to help the poor and the needy,
to be at the service of your neighbor, to be completely engaged in the secular world—this is what authentic prayer
amounts to. If to work is to pray, so also to run is to pray—
currere est orare—in other words, my total involvement in
secular affairs can also be the vehicle of my prayer and my
whole religious life. I do not need to go apart from the
secular world in order to pray; my prayer is made through
my secular involvement in all its dimensions.

I can see and sympathize with the point of this post-
Vatican II "secular Christianity" view of prayer and the
religious life—at least insofar as it exposes the distortions
to which the older view is prone. However, you have to take
yourself as you are, warts and all, and I am afraid that my
point of departure remains a more or less traditional one.
I am prepared to give away a good many of the devotional
practices associated with the older asocial, "confronta-
tional," view of spirituality and to discard a good deal of its
mythology; but I am also convinced that there is a central
truth in the whole tradition that runs from the Desert
Fathers to Charles de Foucauld and St. Thérèse of Lisieux
that remains valid even in these latter days of grace. In this
respect at least, I am, like Paul Goodman in another context, content to be seen as a "neolithic conservative." I
know that I am spitting into the wind of the Christian
Zeitgeist, but I cannot help it and I am not much
concerned.

I think all this came home to me last year when I spent some time in a kind of personal "retreat" at the ancient Benedictine abbey of Bec-Hellouin in France. Having written a book on St. Anselm of Bec, I went to the abbey to pay my pious respects to the memory of the saint, and remained to pray. The monks and the nuns keep up the liturgical offices very beautifully at Bec-Hellouin, and it is taken for granted that the main work of the place is prayer and contemplation just as it was in the 12th century when Lanfranc and Anselm were there. After a few days, all this seemed perfectly natural and real to me and rumors of war and revolution, hijackings, Watergate, the environment crisis, became insubstantial and faded into the background. Inside the abbey the most important and real thing was that the liturgical offices be said, and that people pray and contemplate and praise God.

While I was at Bec-Hellouin one of the sisters lent me a book called *Living Prayer* by Anthony Bloom, a Russian Orthodox archbishop. Bloom's book sums up and crystallizes very beautifully the whole classical stream of Christian spirituality; as I read it at Bec it seemed to be perfectly right and apt. And yet, once again, there is hardly a word in Bloom's essay about issues of social justice in the secular world: For him the life of the spirit is quite distinct from the life of secular involvement.

At all events, I found myself, almost to my surprise, more and more sympathetic to the whole climate at Bec-Hellouin and to the order of priority of values, as they say, that obtained there. I think, in a sense, that I became clearly aware for the first time of my own personal religious "style" or "vocation." In a kind of "great thoughts" journal that I keep spasmodically, I wrote the following note at the time:

"Whatever else is uncertain, this is where I must begin from, this is my personal 'bench mark.' I am convinced that the ancient conception of the spiritual life—despite the misleading categories used to describe it—retains a kernel of value. I cannot now agree with A.C. [an American friend] that the traditional conception of prayer and the religious life was bound up with a quasi-Cartesian 'anthropology' according to which the 'real' self is identified with the private asocial self, and thinking and contemplation are seen as superior to action in the material world. I know that there is a great problem here—how to reconcile contemplation and action, prayer with secular concern and involvement, the inner and the social self. But I also know that my personal 'style' or 'vocation' is to try to bring about this reconciliation, to begin building the bridge, from this end."

What I have said so far makes me sound rather like a latter-day "Little Flower," a kind of spiritual antiquarian. Perhaps it may have some more point if I say that my "secular" life is, and always has been, one of frenetic activity, and again, that I have been immersed in social action of various kinds for many years. Some weeks before I went to Bec-Hellouin, indeed, I had been at a peace conference in Utrecht in Holland with people like Dom Helder Camara, Thich Nat Hanh, the Abbe Pierre—all anguished about the radical injustices that exist in the world and all concerned to stress how the demands of social justice are central to Christianity and to any religion. There at Utrecht it was tempting to solve the problem of how to reconcile prayer with action by identifying the two and by making prayer and the spiritual life consist wholly in one's social action in the secular world. To help the needy, to stand with the oppressed, to suffer with the suffering, to practice non-violence *is* to be united with God, *is* to pray.

However, none of the men I have just mentioned, Helder Camara, Thich Nat Hanh, the Abbe Pierre, make this identification, and neither can I. It is right to protest against the distortions introduced into the religious life by a dualistic separation of the private, interior life of prayer from one's action and involvement in the world of secular values; but it also seems to me that it is an equal and opposite error to identify the two. (There is an analogy here with the philosophical problem of the relationship between the mind and the body. The dualist like Descartes separates mind and body so strictly that they can never have any commerce; while the behaviorist, in his zeal to expose the inadequacies of the dualist, ends by identifying the mind with our bodily behavior *sans plus*. And just as dualist and behaviorist keep themselves respectively in business by scoring off each other and pointing to the deficiencies of the other's position, so also the "traditionalists" and the "secular Christians" each keep themselves afloat by pointing at the beam in the other's eye while conveniently neglecting to notice the mote in their own.)

However, quite apart from these theoretical considerations, there is the question of religious "style" or "vocation" which I mentioned before and which is very important as far as I am concerned. Put very crudely, there are, I suppose, two basic and irreducible styles of life or vocations—the vocation of the man who values and cultivates the inner self and personal relationships, and, on the other hand, the vocation of the man who lives in his deeds Reading Gladstone's autobiographical fragments some time ago, I was struck by the peculiar lack of substance, of personal density, of selfhood, that emerged from them. Gladstone's self was, so to speak, absorbed in his deeds and actions, in his social *persona.* Contrast Newman, almost neurotically concerned with the cultivation of his inner self ("those two great luminous beings," as he says in the *Apologia,* "myself and God"), at the cost of being largely ineffectual in his social activity.

Or again, to take a contemporary and secular example, we might compare someone like E. M. Forster with Che Guevara. From what one can gather from his friends' memoirs, Forster put enormous effort into nurturing his own personal substance, cultivating personal density and richness, and giving great importance to intimate personal relationships. Che Guevara, on the other hand, opted for the vocation of social action and literally gave his own self —gave up having a self—for others. Reading Che Guevara's writings I find it difficult to grasp any person behind them; he lives in other people, in his deeds.

I don't want to suggest that these two styles of life are strictly exclusive so that you have to choose *either* one *or* the other. Being a Christian, indeed, involves that you must, to some extent, be concerned with both in some way. But I think that each person will have his own emphasis and lean either one way or the other.

In my own case, I certainly feel the pull, and very strongly, of both vocations; but—I suppose it is middle age coming upon me—I am increasingly attracted by the Newman/Forster style of life, even though I am fully aware of the price that has to be paid for this emphasis. I admire the Gladstones and the Che Guevaras of the spiritual life, but I cannot imitate them.

I have gone on at such length about all of this because these kinds of questionings and doubts about prayer and the religious life are as much a part of my own spiritual life as anything else. To run or not to run? How does one reconcile the need to withdraw from the running, from immersion in the secular, in order to "recollect oneself in the presence of God," as the old formula had it, to pray in a face-to-face way with God? How do you reconcile this with a necessary concern with the values of the secular world which, as Teilhard de Chardin has reminded us once for all, is a sacrament of God? In one way or another I have wrestled with these questions ever since I came to the age of religious reason, and I suppose that this is one of the causes of my religious psyche being in such a schizoid state and my religious life being such a mish-mash of old reflexes and habits and spasmodic new experiments.

For instance, I still set great store by something so old fashioned as morning and night prayers. The instinct to flop on my knees by my bed first thing in the morning and last thing at night is, I suppose, almost a conditioned reflex since it goes back to the dim past of my Catholic upbringing. "A man may be a fornicator and a drunkard and a murderer," our old Irish parish priest used to thunder, "but if he says his morning and evening prayers he can't be wholly damned!"

Even if Father O'Reilly rather over-rated the importance of this simple kind of prayer (one had vivid images of his man reverently saying his prayers just before cheerfully fornicating or murdering!) it is still not to be sneezed at. To a very large extent prayer and the spiritual life is a job of work that just has to be done—nine parts perspiration, as they say, and one part inspiration—and to have routine prayers of this kind is a valuable reminder of the routine, humdrum character of the spiritual life.

Again, I try to set aside some regular time for some kind of more or less formal meditation. I have found most of the advice I have received from the standard Catholic books on prayer, and from the standard Catholic priest, pretty useless on the practice of prayer and meditation. Like many pious books on how to make love, most books on how to pray are too vague and general to be much help (though I must except here Archbishop Bloom's little book *Living Prayer*). One thing I am sure of is that it doesn't come naturally or spontaneously; it must be practiced like swimming or tennis or playing the piano, and it must be encouraged and supported by a good deal of theological reflection and study.

It seems to me that our images of God and our relationships to God continually need criticism and purification. We play sado-masochistic games with God just as we do with our wives and husbands and lovers, and we need to perform a continual auto-critique on our spiritual life. To my mind, this kind of critical reflection is just as much a part of my religious life as anything else.

In my own case, this has been very much influenced by a couple of visits to Japan which allowed me some fleeting contact with Buddhism and Shintoism. I had always been suspicious of the "wisdom of the mysterious East" and of the Eastern religious syncretism of popular sages like Aldous Huxley and Alan Watts, and I suppose I was pretty much the ordinary Christian chauvinist. However, two experiences in Japan made me dramatically aware of the fact that Christianity is simply a species of the genus religion and that, while it is not true that all religions are one, there is never-theless a profound oneness in the religious impulse. Taking part in an exquisitely beautiful Shinto service in Kyoto, for instance, I became vividly conscious of how much—despite the abysses of cultural and religious difference between us—we were all about basically the same business, doing basic-ally the same job. Again, walking in the grounds of the Buddhist monastery of Nanzen-ji, and hearing a gong and a flute playing within the monastery I suddenly felt "at home." I knew what the monks were about. This simple, almost trite, experience had an enormous effect upon me.

As a Christian I view my own religious tradition as being in some way central and paradigmatic, but the awareness that there are other possible ways (and very noble ways at that) has helped to purge my own view of God and of the religious life of parochialism and tribalism and superstition. After Japan, my conception of the God I confront in prayer and meditation is a much less specifically "Catholic" one, and I think that it is all the more religious and all the more Christian because of that.

I mentioned before that there was precious little advice to be had about the practice of meditation. I have come more and more to realize the need for techniques in the spiritual life, and yet in the tradition of Western Chris-tianity there has been curiously little concern with the practical means and devices of being religious. In a fascinat-ing essay on "Techniques of the Body," the great French ethnologist Marcel Mauss (the intellectual father of Claude Lévi-Strauss) says that "at the bottom of all our mystical states there are techniques of the body which we have not studied, but which were perfectly studied by China

and India, even in very remote periods." No doubt there
has been a justified fear in Western Christianity that the
religious life should not become a matter of gymnastics (the
subject of an ABC of spiritual techniques rather like the
"ABC of love"). God is not subject to man's devices and
tricks, and religion and religious experience can no more
be called up by the appropriate techniques than can love.

But, allowing for these possible abuses, we have done very
little, compared with Eastern religions, to analyze the practical means of meditation and prayer. After all, if human
love requires the learning of bodily techniques, so also does
the love of God. I have read Fr. Dechanet's *Christian Yoga*
and I have tried some of the means described by Archbishop
Bloom—praying in unison with breathing, repeating a
"Divine Name" over and over, etc.—but I wish I knew a
lot more about all this. As R. C. Zaehner has put it: At a
time when so many young people are looking for some kind
of religious initiation, the Christian churches seem to have
almost nothing to offer in this field. The churches talk about
the "social gospel" and "secular Christianity" and the
"death of God" while the young go off to meditate with the
Hare Krishna movement, or the Divine Light, or to seek
illumination through pop Zen or Leary-style drug mysticism.
(I suppose that this is one of the things that attracts some
people to the Pentecostalist or Charismatic movement—
it offers a practical technique for praying. My own tempera-
ment is such, however, that I don't think I could ever join
the Pentecostals. Like Bishop Butler I find that kind of
religious enthusiasm "a very horrid thing," though I am
willing to live and let live.)

I have been speaking as though prayer and meditation
and the cultivation of the spiritual life had nothing to do

with my life in the church, in the Christian community to which I belong. In concrete terms, how do the Eucharist and the sacraments fit in with the life I have just been describing? I must say honestly that I do not see clearly how they fit in, although I know what the received theological view is and although I am a regular Mass goer and sacrament frequenter. I have nothing against public rites —indeed I think they are absolutely necessary if religion is not to evaporate into sentimentality (the so-called "religion of the heart" usually ends up being a religion of the viscera) —but in some strange way the present rites we have in the church seem to be out of phase with our religious needs. They are no longer religiously expressive, though I find it hard to be more specific about this. Most young people, at any rate, seem to find them irrelevant and without meaning, and some at least find the pop Eastern religions more in tune with their religious yearnings.

I said before that I felt like a "neolithic conservative" in my approach to prayer and the spiritual life, so much does it seem to be out of harmony with the prevailing spirit of the times in the church. (The very terms in which I have been speaking here about prayer and meditation and the spiritual life echo an older religious fashion.) And yet there are small but real signs of a turning away from "social gospel" Christianity, from *praxis* Christianity, toward a more traditional contemplative or visionary view. Even though it manifests itself in some bizarre forms—Jesus Freaks, LSD mysticism, Beat Zen, certain modes of Pentecostalism—this tendency to a revival of what has been called "ecstatic religion" is, I believe, a real and deep one. Whatever one may think of the gurus of the counterculture —Theodore Roszak and others of that ilk—there is no doubt that their attacks on the "objective consciousness" of our science and technoculture (impersonal, quantitative, utilitarian, exploitative modes of thinking) and their exaltation of mystical and imaginative forms of consciousness strike a deep chord in many people's religious psyches at the present time. This change in religious outlook and attitude is, I believe, part of a more fundamental shift that is now taking place in our whole cultural "structure" and in the interpretative schemas and perspectives that are a function of it—a shift toward a quasi-aesthetic view of reason and of its relation to nature, as against the activist and exploitative technological view that emerged from the Industrial Revolution; a shift toward contemplation and vision and imagination, as against the cult of the naked will and of action that came from Kant and the Enlightenment; toward a morality of sensitivity and perception and of the cultivation of the "inner self" as against the morality of utilitarianism.

As Paul Goodman has suggested, if one's conservativism is "neolithic" enough, there is a good chance that it will turn out to be tomorrow's radicalism. With a little bit of luck, then, I may soon be in the spiritual avant-garde.

WHERE TO BEGIN?

JOHN GARVEY is an editor for Templegate Publishing Company. After graduating from Notre Dame he taught, served in the public information department at Sangamon State University, and for three years edited University Today, *an education newsletter. His book reviews have appeared in* The Critic *and* Commonweal, *and he is the author of the forthcoming* Contemporary Meditations on the Saints *(Thomas More Press). Mr. Garvey, his wife and their two children make their home in Springfield, Illinois.*

by John Garvey

THERE IS A STORY THAT CHARLES DARWIN LOST HIS FAITH ON seeing the jungle coast of South America. He saw something new about the world, a world in which until that moment he might have felt comfortable. Now it was no longer a world he could imagine; it was *wild,* and the world in which he had believed was not. So something was lost: an absolute sense of what the world was about. But the shaking-up which this vision caused could also be seen as an invitation to enter a much richer world.

Something similar is happening today. Until a few years years ago the majority of Christians felt more or less comfortable in their own religious traditions. Quite a few, no doubt, still feel that way. But something new has happened in the lives of many people. It is not necessarily that they have lost faith, but they have the feeling that faith and its demands are not what they had assumed. They are unsure of the church and its role in their lives. Yet the words and person of Jesus stay with them, and they believe that the church is in some uncomfortable way a tradition in which they must live and worship. There is literally nowhere else to go.

Are there any alternatives? First of all, I would not want to say that only those who suffer from a mood of uncertainty have anything to tell us, or that they are always the "new wave." It is not as if everyone who has a disturbed sense of things had seen something as striking as the jungle coast. But I think *some* have, and for the rest of us—if we are attentive—this emptiness, this sense of loss, can be an invitation to enter a richer world, a world created by a God who is not made in our image.

Gandhi suggested that we might reverse the statement "God is Truth" to read "Truth is God." There is an implication here that we do not know what God is, that God, like truth, is discovered and disclosed during the course of a life, and is not a thing we "have" or "do not have." The discovery of this truth, of the real world, involves prayer; and the degree to which a person considers prayer important is the degree to which he is serious about his life. Unless the sense men have had in every age—that life is based in something sacred—is false, this is our first work. The question, "How do you live the life of prayer in the modern world?" is not simply part of a greater religious problem. It has everything to do with the meaning of our lives. This is the problem—in theory. And that's the easy part. The *real* problem is, how does anyone begin?

I think you are handed your ideas about these things by a community, more than you choose them. That community may (as in the case of churchgoing believers) be some definitely religious structure. It may (as in the case of those who find themselves religious to their great surprise, like some converts to Quakerism I know) be a "found" community, one encountered in random meetings, or

through reading . . . wholly by accident. But the decisions
you make about these things are formed by the people who
have known you.

I grew up in a home which allowed arguments about religion. I don't know how rare that is, but I remember (for
example) my father telling us that the teacher who said
that sin makes God unhappy was simply wrong, that
nothing could get in the way of God's joy. I'm sure my
parents didn't intend this result, but I never felt very bitter
about the more obvious shortcomings of the church because
I never expected much of it in the first place. I mean the
church as an institution: We were taught that the saints
were on to something, but I think I read their lives the way
I read science fiction and fairy tales; they were adventures.
The sacraments were important in our home, and we knew
it didn't matter if the priest administering them was a fool.
The church was made up of people who were, on the average . . . well, *average*. To expect more would be foolish. It
was the gospels, saints, and sacraments that mattered. Religion had more to do with illumination and discovery than
with morality and restriction, though I suppose we suffered ordinary and maybe not unfruitful problems with
those categories. I'm sure, anyway, that all of this influenced
the direction in which I looked for answers.

One way or another it led to a rather comfortable belief
in what I can only call "the God of Comparative Religion."
This was not a God who might be thought of as seeking
man, or one who could conceivably make demands. It was
something vague and benign and cosmic. It was also too
much like what *I* would want God to be, if I were in charge
of creating God—definitely a God made in my image and

likeness. (There are several ways to react to this pass. One is the way chosen by some unpleasant fundamentalists who preach a God so awful, so indecent, that he must be at least as real as rape or murder. I've seen comic books distributed by Jesus Freaks, accounts of hell and its horrors, which make the worst nuns' tales pale.)

About this time I read Pascal's account of his strange visitation—he described it as *fire*—and his belief that this was not "the God of the philosophers" but "the God of Abraham, Isaac, and Jacob." The Catholic version of unitarianism I'd wound up in was an obvious dead end, and—very skeptically—I began to attend Catholic Pentecostal meetings. I lost some of the skepticism because there were many prayerful and good people there whose lives had benefited from contact with Pentecostalism. But in another respect the skepticism was reinforced. Whatever claims they might make, I felt that Pentecostals depended far too much on "special effects"—tongues, prophecy, and so forth. A friend later wrote to me that he found them "too bright-eyed and fascist," and he's right about at least some of them. The major problem for me, I think, was a total incapacity for the sort of conviction they demanded. They were too much like the "saved" who always make me uncomfortable. Their assurance seemed unhealthy, too ripe. I don't deny that during the course of history some people have had utterly convincing encounters with the divine. But it couldn't be the basis of an honest spiritual life to keep hoping that you will be visted by an angel or knocked off a horse. To aim at a convincing experience makes the search for truth secondary to a search for personal conviction and consolation.

I came to believe answers aren't that easily come by, and the ones we are offered, have to be approached not as ends but as beginnings. But in trying to offer a sense of where I have been looking I also have to offer an apology. I am as erratic about attention to these things as the next person; but what non-adepts have to say may be valuable. They may be able to offer help where a lot of traditional writing fails—if only because so much writing about prayer seems to have been written by angels; it has little in common with the real texture of the lives led by the people who turn to it for help.

The sort of spirituality which could speak to my condition would have to be addressed to someone doubtful, a condition which I know I share with a lot of people. It would not aim at demolishing doubt (that wouldn't work) but rather at helping to create the space needed for prayer and meditation. It would treat doubt not as a completely negative phenomenon, but as the beginning of an important openness—the acknowledgement that you do not know where you are being led. Such a spirituality would mean showing people what you know of the way, and what you believe can be discovered, rather than trying to convince them of something which you yourself really doubt.

Prayer has always involved uncertainty about what we are and what God is, and it has always involved discovery. Any look at the contentions between spiritual directors and those they directed, whether they occurred in the stark settlements of the desert fathers or in Zen monasteries, will reveal the fact that complacency has never been a sign of spiritual depth. Visions of a past peace could be misleading. If there is anything new in our condition it is that cultural and social props which once were unchallenged have now been severely shaken.

But there *are* some authorities, and they are especially important in an uncertain time. Every religious tradition which has lasted more than a few hundred years has arrived at curiously similar conclusions regarding progress in the spiritual life. All have, to some degree, admitted the need for spiritual direction, some form of simple living or asceticism, and disciplined meditation—a process of self-emptying and concentration. Most important, all of them agree that such a life is not to be followed because it fulfills us on an individual basis or is good therapy, but because it has to do with the way the universe is constituted, with the reasons we are here. (In this respect the decline of monasticism in Catholic consciousness may have consequences we haven't foreseen yet. Though it will give us more in common with Protestant Christians, it weakens our ties with the religions of the East. This is something Thomas Merton saw. It is interesting that he, a *monk* of all things, had such a profound influence on his lay contemporaries. In recent years he has found a newer and younger audience, perhaps because of his interest in Eastern religion and his ability to translate its meaning for Western readers.)

One of my assumptions—and I plead guilty—is that if, after centuries of cultural meditation involving thousands of people experienced in prayer and meditation, traditions as diverse in origin as Christianity and Buddhism arrive at startlingly similar conclusions about the way people who are serious about such things should live, I should listen. The natural history of the human animal seems to be speaking as authoritatively as anything could.

While it is true that a number of people feel no urgency to move in this direction, I wonder whether it is possible to feel the urgency of the life of prayer before you get some idea of what Paul meant about longing for deliverance from the body of this death. Those who would claim that such a bleak starting point is "life-denying" are working out of a protected space which probably won't be protected for long. They have to contend with the insights of Gautama Buddha, who was moved to seek enlightenment after encounters with old age, suffering, and death; with Socrates, who called the love of wisdom the practice of dying; with Jesus, who wept at Lazarus' death and felt "dismay and horror" at Gethsemane, before his abandonment. In an age which has seen Hitler's camps, Vietnam, Biafra, the slaughter of Indians in Latin America, the deaths of those so poor they can't move away from flood or famine, and the daily fact of our own dying, it should be obvious that the *memento mori*, the skull in the Carthusian's cell, the meditation of Buddhist monks on the stages of decomposition, all have more to do with what life is about than the comparative shallowness of *I'm OK—You're OK* and *Psychology Today*.

I suppose this comes down to a kind of radical traditionalism. Men can't worship without a tradition any more than they can speak without a language. And it isn't possible to extract the "best" from all religions, as if you had a perspective from which such things could be judged. (Anyone who believed he did have such a perspective would probably be assuming the correctness of some currently fashionable worldview. He might dismiss or underestimate the asceticism which most mystical traditions have in common, since asceticism is unfashionable. He would find ritual relatively unimportant, and see every instance in which compassion is recommended as a sign of enlightened thinking. In other words, he would unwittingly be working out of a strain of thinking offered him by Judaeo-Christian tradition to reject other, less fashionable things to be found in this and in every other major religious tradition.)

Simone Weil wrote: "The Catholic tradition contains explicitly truths which other religions contain implicitly. But conversely, other religions contain explicitly truths which are only implicit in Christianity. The most well-informed Christian can still learn a great deal concerning divine matters from other religious traditions, although inward spiritual light can also cause him to apprehend everything through the medium of his own tradition. All the same, were these other traditions to disappear from the face of the earth it would be an irreparable loss. The missionaries have already made far too many of them disappear as it is."

It is people like Weil, and Gandhi, and Merton, whose vision can indicate a way for the rest of us. It is the sort of thing they discovered which could be like Darwin's vision of the jungle coastline—unsettling, but an invitation into a greater world. It is a spirituality, a catholicity, open enough to include truths found in new places and other traditions. Gandhi's understanding of Hinduism and the Bhagavad-Gita, its most popular scripture, was enriched by his contact with the New Testament. Merton's understanding of Christianity and of his own monastic vocation was illuminated by his study of Buddhism. Simone Weil remained outside of any particular religious tradition, believing that she could separate herself from none of them and that she must therefore be a kind of exile from all. But she wrote more acutely of Christianity than anyone has since. A vital point is that while none of them made an idol of tradition, and all made some distinction between popular, "respectable" religion and the tradition which popular religion often exploits, all of them realized that traditional understandings are central to the life of the spirit.

Reinterpreting traditions in order to make them more attractive won't solve anything or restore anything. No one converts to an interpretation of anything; no one's life has been changed by talk about how the Christian "symbol system" sheds light on the way we already live anyway. Such talk is important, but not to the work of living, or prayer.

A person interested in beginning could start with Weil, or Gandhi, or Merton. There are hundreds of other things: *The Practice of the Presence of God,* by Brother Lawrence; the anonymous *Way of a Pilgrim;* the desert fathers; John of the Cross; C. S. Lewis; and these can be reinforced by readings from other religions, like the Bhagavad-Gita or the Upanishads. It is important, in any event, not to assume the irrelevance of traditional spirituality. Many of these books are, like the scriptures or great secular classics, in the "either you see it or you don't" category.

Most people—including me—are afraid to do what this life, accepted single-mindedly, would demand. The demands seem simple enough; they involve setting aside time, allowing yourself to realize some silence. It is work, and there is no way to make it constantly pleasant, but it is also rest. One metaphor which crops up in every tradition is that of the pond which is allowed to settle, so that the water becomes clear. Prayer is a waiting in which things become clear. That may be why we avoid it. Our fear comes from what may be demanded of us: We may have to change.

Is there any uniquely modern problem about living such a life? I think so. The times during which people are alone with themselves have diminished considerably. (When people walked to and from work, the walk imposed a kind of silence. Now we have car radios.) A meditative state of mind can impose itself in moments of silence. We distract ourselves at every opportunity, and the opportunities have multiplied.

Beyond this there is the assumption that prayer must be made to fit into the rest of living, rather than the other way around. It might be good in some cases to encourage a variety of dropping out. Where our work is obsessive to the point of near-madness it may be that there is nothing which can be done but to leave it. If somehow we can do that "in place," fine. If by rearranging things, by creating time, we can stay where we are and see more clearly we will be doing well. But some people don't seem to be able to do this. It may be a kind of puritanism or pride which keeps them from admitting it. An ad executive or a university president, for example, may honestly believe that he is somehow a force for good in his present position. But if his way of living distorts his perceptions, if he finds it difficult or impossible to pray, if his efforts to take a reasonable and proportioned view of himself and his work fail repeatedly, perhaps he should question his assumption.

In *Free in Obedience*, William Stringfellow identifies demonic principalities and powers with the ways in which people can be "taken over"—by their own images (as in the case of Hitler) or by institutions like Bell Telephone or ITT. Many of us know people who were changed by their work, who became less as they grew more involved in the obsessions which institutional politics can engender. "It must increase, and I must decrease." Perhaps they could not have done otherwise, given what they were obliged to accept in order to continue working at all, what they were obliged to become to themselves, their families, and others —what, finally, they were obliged to serve. People as diverse as the Catholic Worker movement, southern agrarians, Paul Goodman, and libertarians on the right and left both, have seen facets of this problem. I would argue that this really is an obstacle—maybe the major one—to living the spiritual life in our time. Everyone assumes that Mammon must be taken care of first, and Mammon is not necessarily as obvious a villain as Hitler or ITT. It could also be the Movement or the Archdiocese of Chicago—any allegiance which serves illusion by allowing us (even encouraging us) to worship false images of God or of ourselves.

Disillusionment in the root sense of the word is the end of the spiritual life. In order to lose false images of God and of ourselves we need to create the space and time necessary to allow things to assume their true shapes. We may find ourselves happily surprised. That, anyway, is the thrust of Christian faith. For Christians the spiritual life means looking for—or waiting for—the kingdom of God, the signs of God's reign. The generosity of God is the source of everything which makes Christianity unique, from prayer to ethics. Peter's first confession of sin in Luke's gospel follows, not remorse over his own sinfulness, but a manifestation of God's awesome generosity. "Leave me, Lord, sinner that I am," he says—when the nets are full.

This generosity is not at all obvious. Paul said that our age has been twisted away from its true pattern; Jesus spoke of the prince of this world. It takes attention and deliberation to arrive at any clarity. I tend to distract myself from that attention almost every time I get the chance. But I do believe that it is necessary. I am probably too fond of several false gods to put them to the test with any intensity or frequency.

But there is no mystery about what I *should* do. It is clear enough, and it has always been there, in Brother Lawrence, the American Quaker John Woolman, John of the Cross, Eckhart, the gospels, and in countless other places East and West. Whatever sanity anyone has comes from proximity to it (granting that such proximity may not always be consciously sought), and any degree of distance makes a life that much less real.

BUILDING THE COMMUNITY

MARGERY FRISBIE is the mother of eight children. To shield her children from her natural penchant for preaching, she has, over the years, vented her views on marriage to Marriage *readers, on children's books to* National Catholic Reporter *readers and on family life to the readers of* Chicago's New World. *The Frisbies live in a suburb of Chicago.*

by Margery Frisbie

ONE EVENING RECENTLY, AS THREE GENERATIONS OF OUR family exchanged stories of their misspent youth over multiple pots of tea, I told how once my brother and I had kept our grandmother imprisoned in a bedroom for the better part of an afternoon.

"Did you really?" our middle daughter asked in disbelief. Ellen credits the naughty tales of her youth, but not mine.

I admitted the story, like most of the rest we'd told, was slightly exaggerated. My grandmother had actually locked herself in, after her afternoon nap, by jerking the doorknob off in her hand. What my brother and I had done was open and shut an adjacent door, shouting, "There's no one here. Isn't that funny? I'm sure I heard a knock," while she whacked thunderously at the door which had shut her in.

"After all," I absolved myself, "she was a very domineering woman. Whenever Bud and I played bridge or pinochle with her, she bid every hand so she could play it, no matter what cards she held. She had to run everything.

"Once she stamped the stool to my new dressing table to pieces over some indignity she suffered. I wasn't responsible for that and it was the only new bedroom set I ever got in my whole life."

The conversation turned to deplorable phone jokes, Ellen's vice, and my anecdote was forgot. But the next morning I could still hear me rerunning my old excuses, my worn rationalization for my execrable behavior that long ago afternoon, and I repented.

Ashamed of my alibi, I sought Ellen out to tell her that her uncle and I had been a nasty pair of kids on occasion and that one of the occasions was the day we refused to release our grandmother.

I don't know how responsible we were for what we did. Elizabeth Savage suggests in *The Last Night at the Ritz* that children aren't cruel. "They just don't know." There's truth to that.

Looking back I'd have to wonder why Bud and I frustrated that old woman. Certainly she'd frustrated us enough. But we accepted that as part of life until Fate, through a worn-out doorknob, played into our hands. True, we took advantage of the opportunity. Part meanness, part high spirits, part insensitivity.

For we couldn't put ourselves in our grandmother's shoes. She was too much "other" for us. Too old, too well-to-do with her Cadillac initialed CTR on the door, too unmoved by our needs, too self-willed.

On our side we were too much turned in on ourselves, too young, too thoughtless, too inexperienced, too brash, perennially put down. Too disinclined to wonder why we did what we did beyond the surface explanation that for once we had the upper hand and it wouldn't hurt to wave it a little.

Now, middle-aged, it is not my daily business to torment myself with the vagaries of that twelve-year-old nor even with those of the woman I am today. Yet I must reflect on that skinny preteen, who was full of doubts and divine discontent one moment and of saucy highjinks the next, to discover what about her will help me understand my own twelve-year-old, what about her will help me understand the me who was once twelve, what about her will help me understand the meaning of life.

I know who I locked in the bedroom then. Who am I locking in a room today? Myself? My husband? My children? My mother? My friends?

I am looking at that twelve-year-old, and everywhere, for wisdom, the compensation promised the middle-aged for their losses.

No longer can I live on the borrowed wisdom of my early years. That insecure twelve-year-old who badgered her grandmother was so hungry for meaning that she swallowed the whole whale of the church at her first encounter with it that year in a parochial school.

She has lived off its provender these intervening years, nourished by its meat and slowly excising its blubber. But only slowly, for her need was great and continued to be great under the pressure to conform, "to be perfect as the Heavenly Father is perfect," to have the stipulated 7.7 children.

Part of the price of conforming was chronic pregnancy. Is it surprising that I found myself astonishing the somewhat sophisticated seniors at Mundelein College with the information that I could bear the frenzied pattern of my days with five preschool children by thinking of them as five little Christs, one spitting up, one climbing up, one throwing up, one up-ended and another upset by the general uproar?

About the time I brought my fifth baby home from St.

Francis Hospital, I answered queries about how things were going by admitting cheerily that there were "never more than two crying, never less than one."

They were tumultuous times and if thinking my youngsters were little Christs was a crutch, it was a support I needed to limp through the days. There was little time then to measure what the church taught against what life was teaching me. It was one of the many times in my life when I had to promise myself, like Scarlet O'Hara, that I would think about everything tomorrow. What I had come to believe was the right course in a quieter moment would have to sustain me until I had the leisure to reconsider.

But if looking at my children as little Christs was twisting doctrine a little, what about the other strains of my belief? Without the handles of the beatitudes, the gospels, the story of the good Samaritan, the knowledge of St. John's dark night of the soul, the prayer of St. Francis to put love where there is no love, what grasp would I have had on dealing with that multiplication of the Frisbies?

I'd started out married life "priest-ridden," Richard, my husband, teased me. Expecting to be expecting, accepting that I must be accepting. Having read in *Praying While You Work* that a wife should bow to her husband's will, even when she thinks it unreasonable, I strove to be the obedient wife. "So if you have vowed before God to obey a husband who turns out to be stupid, misinformed and prejudiced," Dom von Zeller cautioned, "be careful how you handle the argument about what is the only thing to do. You're really being wise if you bow to him."

When I consistently obeyed against my judgment (who's to say it was better but it was mine), I stood accused of having "snits." I tried not to show them—I remember my maternal grandfather pleading with his wife not to give him "the silent treatment"—but I wasn't successful.

Whenever a decision had to be made, Richard and I would mull over the right and wrong of it, but from my point of view it was ultimately the might of it that made the difference. I was left with the Zellerite admonition to accept my marching orders and get moving.

Somehow I couldn't help resenting the high-handedness of the ukases, getting angry, turning the anger in on myself and, lo!, a fit of depression. A snit.

Knowing the depression would gradually lighten, I tried like the Little Flower not to inflict my feelings on anyone else. I shut my mouth as I'd been taught, threw clothes in the washer, poked them in the dryer, slathered peanut butter on whole wheat toast, piled the painted blocks in the painted boxes, all the while muttering "My Jesus mercy" a hundred times a minute.

If a mantra helps release worries and concerns and aggressive thoughts, I guess my Roman Catholic mantra pushed my aggressions deeper into my gut. They certainly didn't disappear.

Even that wasn't all bad. I could have taken my disaffection out on my children by beating them up, on my neighbors by ragging them, and on my husband by nagging him. But another part of my "religion," my value system, was the belief that I shouldn't nag (saying anything twice is nagging at our house), should not yell nor hit my children and should be kind to neighbors and make them casseroles when they were ailing.

Picture the little stick Catholic, saying "My Jesus mercy," fetching and carrying at home and helping out neighbors as best I could. Something had to give.

Fortunately one of my friends was horrified to hear that I kept my cool by drenching myself in little aspirations. She announced bluntly that I was a damn fool and that I better busy myself finding out what I was pushing down that wanted to come erupting, burbling, bursting up.

"You've got to remember that your great St. Teresa advised that there are some things that can't be changed, but there are some things that can be. You don't have to grin and bear everything," she said. "Nor weep and 'My Jesus mercy' everything either."

She recommended that I create the leisure to go look about instead of waiting until the time presented itself, and use it to see how I could manage to make a little room in the nest for myself without pushing out any of the people I lived with. She thought, for goodness sake, that I should take my feelings into account.

She sugested I also think about where I was going and what it all meant.

By this time I had some credit in the bank with Richard. He no longer dreaded he might wake one morning and find I'd metamorphosed into *his* domineering grandmother.

Would you call it a general confession? As I tried to figure out what was going on inside me, I'd confide in Richard although he's very queasy about viewing anyone's psychic innards. He'd pooh-pooh some and tell people at parties that his wife was going off the deep end when she expressed her dramatic discoveries about the nature of man and woman, of the church.

But I persisted, trying not to drag on too much but expounding as best I could each new understanding I achieved, many of them, as Archibald MacLeish once said, things I'd known were true at twenty but that I couldn't possibly have guessed were as true as they were, "true with a brutal and inescapable truthfulness and consequence and meaning which would have shocked [me] had [I] guessed at it years before."

There was no assigning blame. The silliest part of the women's movement, it seems to me, is the underlying notion that the bulk of men are off having a rinky-tink good time while the women are home slaving. Not that many women are slaving any harder than their breadwinners.

Husbands are not to blame, nor is the church. I'm persuaded that I, and others like me, are the church. If I was in throes, then the church was in throes. As a matter of fact the church during those pre-Vatican II and Vatican II days was self-searching just as I was. I was influenced by its convulsions and the church, to some little extent, was necessarily jarred by mine.

At some time, surely, we had instituted every pious practice suggested in the liturgical revival. We said family prayers in the living room together on our knees and we have a photograph Ed Lettau took for the *Sign* magazine to prove it. (It's a measure of the swiftness of the changes that our younger children don't know what it is ever to kneel. They've only worshiped in a parish center where we stand or sit on bang-bang folding chairs.)

Richard and I said (and sang!) Compline together every night. We devised paraliturgical celebrations for feast days, holy days, birthdays, aniversaries. We decorated the Pentecost cake with strawberry halves for tongues of fire, hid three beans in the Epiphany cake, kept a box of holy props for all occasions—a dove for confirmation, model infantry-men made in Britain for soldiers of Christ, the holder for the Advent wreath.

Some of the rituals, like our lovely family dinner on Holy Thursday for which Richard blesses matzos and wine and reads the "I will not leave you friendless" passage, we can never discontinue. There were terrible complaints the year Margaret was born during Holy Week and I couldn't keep both engagements.

Our painful rendering of the Gelineau version of "Give Thanks to the Lord/ For He is Good," which we use as a grace at dinner, is classically off-key. But now indispensable.

The church has been a mother to us. She has been a mother to me. If, now, I stand off and criticize some, it's not that I love her any less. Only, perhaps, more maturely, more wisely.

When I needed the church to shore up my insufficiency, to make sense of a confusing world, to give me direction, to provide a haven for my waywardness, to protect me from bungling relationships, she was firm in what was expected of me, and generous in giving me people who cared to help.

Then, like any good mother, she let me search out new meanings without disinheriting me. I am persuaded, like Simone Weil who says of the church that its mysteries are "an inexhaustible source of truths concerning the human condition," that when one is pursuing deeper understanding one should dig into one's own tradition. One's sensibilities, one's vocabulary, one's tics and pulses, habits of life, one's customary hold on the verities, all ease one's own access to truth.

My feeling of being at home in Ireland last fall was certainly a measure of my unconscious, atavistic sympathy with the culture of those who offered me tea before their peat fires and tucked a hot water bottle at my feet. I had more possibility of coming to the truth in them and the truth in me in the land of Tara than in any more alien land.

Why would I look elsewhere when I have not yet begun to live out the implications of that sermon which counseled humility and poverty of spirit and the blessedness of mourning? That kind of openness to others' needs that Jesus preached is still a challenge. The good that I would do I still don't do. I tend to inflate myself when I should be reaching out to others.

But that doesn't keep me from thinking I'm religious. At a recent convention of the laity, a young professor from Catholic University began a session on religious development in the home by asking the participants to imagine they were going to have an extra week in New Orleans after the convention because of a transportation shut-down.

There would be no way to leave the city, Dr. Andrew Thompson told the audience, and no communication out of it. "You would have a week to do absolutely anything you wished, with no obligations to anyone. Take three minutes and consider what you would do. Sightsee? Visit the famous French Quarter? Go to the library and read? Try some of the fabled restaurants? Shop in the outdoor market?

"Look at your list," he asked the participants after three minutes had passed, "and see which activities you listed are religious. Who decided to attend daily mass? Use the time for spiritual reading? Visit the religious shrines in the city?"

Whatever choices I had made I would have answered that my choices were religious because they were all concerned with an assignment of value (Dr. Thompson's point). Discerning values is a religious practice. It is by discerning values and facing facts that we come to meaning.

But over and above what we can discover by straining our minds and our emotions to find meaning, there seems to be another way of coming to fulfilled living that is known to the mystics of many faiths.

Hints of it are all around us. Teilhard insisted that there was something afoot in the universe. The mystics tell us that our vocation is "waiting on God"; this is not an effort of the will, Simone Weil reminds us, but an "unremitting, patient, single-minded attentiveness," a motionless expectancy directed to His presence.

I know something like that. When a person has been forced to wake from his dreams night after night, researchers tell us, he is finally so hungry to dream that he dreams constantly all through his sleeping period. Somewhat the same way, I find that when my attention has too long been focused on the minutiae of life, that I cannot sit down in a chair or open a book without rising into a suspended state where I don't want to think or read but just be.

Instead of flowing forward, as in a stream of consciousness, I am at rest, attentive perhaps, but submersed in the moment, aware, poised, appreciative, leaning into the essence of life instead of stroking away from it.

Without trying to articulate it, only to experience it, I'm conscious of another dimension beyond the daily, willing to be suspended in it and refreshed by it, grateful for its message of the good.

Looking from the eminence of those moments at woman's choice today, in bald terms, of fulfilling herself or building the eternal city, I incline more to the choice of a Rose in Margaret Drabble's *The Needle's Eye* than to that of Doris Lessing's heroine in *Summer Before the Dark*.

Doris Lessing's character, if I read her right, her role as full-time wife and mother coming to an end, enters into a period of self-discovery, following her impulses to travel, to dally, to manipulate others, to experience countries and persons, searching out meaning and purpose in their interstices.

What I can't understand is that she looks for meaning everywhere but in the life she shared with her husband and children, that life she built with her years and moments, her struggles and concern for them, her daily getting up and lying down. What is the point of freeing ourselves in self-discovery if not to serve freely that world which we served bound? What good is a self-fulfillment that doesn't flow to others?

Rose, in *The Needle's Eye*, having known violent confrontation and the hand of power over her, struggles to build a community, however small, where might doesn't rule. A community where love prevails in service. Her life is symbolized by the old house she tries to restore. "She shivered, she trembled, she flinched, but she persevered, she had faith, she built up brick by brick the holy city of her childhood, the holy city in the shape of that patched, subsiding house. It was slow, it was very slow, but gradually the ideal and the real merged and swam together. . . ."

Rose is a builder, and such must be my longing, for as I was writing this, I had a dream that Richard and I had two extra houses, both modest. I was looking forward to fixing them up and letting people use them.

However, I discovered in my dream that they were already occupied by people whom I had not chosen but who obviously needed them, were cheered to have them and were pleasantly grateful for the opportunity. They weren't overly-grateful; they took their welcome for granted.

I told Richard, twisting the metaphor as is common in dreams, that it was for all the world as if you kept making places in yourself for others and their needs, thinking that you could invite those who would get to slake their thirst at your fountain, so to speak. But the people who would drink there would not be of your choosing. But then again not not of your choosing.

"So you are allowed to give to others," I asked Richard as I told him the dream the next morning, "but not to choose?"

"That is the whole thing, isn't it?" he asked.

"Yes, I suppose so," I agreed slowly; "if my grandmother were here, no doubt she would be moving in."

THERE IS TIME, YET NOT ENOUGH

One of Ireland's leading journalists, DESMOND FISHER specializes in current affairs, economics and religion. He was formerly London Editor of the Irish Press group; *editor of the* Catholic Herald, London, *and a frequent contributor to newspapers and magazines in Europe and the U.S. Author of* The Church in Transition, *he is now head of Current Affairs for Radio Telefís Eireann, the national Irish broadcasting service.*

by Desmond Fisher

I WAS BORN IN DERRY, NORTHERN IRELAND, IN 1920. THAT
information alone should explain much of my background,
including the religious side of it. Even to an American
reader, 3000 or more miles away, Derry—and its Creggan
and Bogside—has become a household word after all the
troubles of the past four or five years.

Growing up in Derry at that time was a process of being
molded by a series of rigid attitudes and prejudices determined exclusively by the religion of one's parents. Religion decided the schools one attended, the friends one
made, the games one played and when one played them,
the stores one shopped in, often the street one lived in. If
your parents were Catholic you went to school to a convent,
the Christian Brothers and St. Columb's. Usually you
played exclusively with other Catholic boys. You played
soccer; the Protestants cricket. You played on Sundays
when the Protestant boys were forbidden to take part in
games and had to wear their Sunday clothes all day while
Catholic boys, or those with vigilant mothers, had changed
into their "old clothes" after mass and breakfast. Catholics
usually dealt with shopkeepers of their own religious per-

suasion and housing allocations were made on a strict denominational basis so that wards could be gerrymandered and a minority Protestant population retain political control of the city. Years later, a new acquaintance or a prospective employer had only to ask you what school you attended or what street you lived in to know all about you and to treat you accordingly.

I was the eldest of three. I do not remember all that much of my earliest years but my mother used to recall the night two policemen knocked at the door and she thought my father would be shot there and then. But they wanted only to tell him he had left a ladder against the gable and burglars might use it. Another night a late reveller ran his walking stick along the iron railings of the front garden and they thought a machine gun was raking the house. Derry was like that in those times.

We lived in West End Park, a decent mixed (i.e. Catholic and Protestant) road overlooking the Bogside. Each morning we walked to school in separate convoys, Catholics to their school, Protestants to theirs. The West End Park children did not fight one another, but we Catholics had to run the gauntlet of Protestants from other areas. The regular game was to try to get first to the walls and gables on which we chalked the slogans, now so familiar on our TV screens, consigning to hell the King on one side and the Pope on the other. Often the slogan-writing turned to fisticuffs and it was an accepted thing to arrive late, dishevelled and bloody-nosed but with the heady conviction of having fought a good fight for the Pope and the Roman Catholic God.

Looking back, I recognize that I was a fairly average product of Irish Catholicism, which is probably too well-known in English-speaking countries to need illustration here. It involved great stress on devotionalism, on masochistic self-denial, on near-superstitious allegiance to seven this and nine that, on a chilling attitude to sex and, above all, on utter dependence on environmental conformity and exclusion of personal responsibility. This form of religion persisted after my family moved to Dublin when I was eleven years old. It was not materially changed by five years in the novitiate of an order, where, with few memorable exceptions, and through no fault of theirs, the priests and brothers were, by today's standards, religiously underdeveloped.

I came out of the order with as little genuine understanding of what it meant to be a Christian as I had going in. But I must have retained, unknown to myself, some marks of years I now wish only to forget, because in 1962, after eighteen years of Irish provincial and national journalism, half of it spent in London, England, I was asked to become editor of the London *Catholic Herald*, a highly-regarded weekly. Almost immediately, I was thrown into the Vatican Council and had the great privilege of being able to cover it almost in full.

It is to the Council and to the devoted priests and bishops who provided the briefings for us journalists that I owe whatever knowledge I have of modern ecclesiological and theological attitudes and understandings. So if in what I write from now on echoes of Vatican II reportage come in, it will be no surprise.

To me, the main point of religion is community. I see mankind as created by God not as a series·of unconnected individuals but as a group of beings who, while possessing individuality, are linked by their common creation, com-

mon substance, common destiny and dependence on one another for their development as persons and as performers of
whatever mission God has created them for. I do not find any
great need of I-Thou relationship with God, though I realize
that this may be a serious flaw in my spirituality. I see my
position rather as that of a member of a group in which I
certainly have an individual role to play but in which the
individual performance is of less account than the totality
of achievement. In other words, I feel that God's view of
me and his calling me to account is concerned not with
how I act individually towards him directly but with my
performance in and for the community of which I am part
and which my divinely-appointed task is to make ever more
community-conscious and community-creating.

The community to which I belong is, of course, not a
static one. Sometimes it is the community of my wife and
myself and my family; at other times that of my relations,
of my friends, of my work-colleagues, of my city or nation
or international grouping. My task in each different community varies according to the particular community I am
being consciously part of at any time. In some communities,
I am a key figure; in others, of lesser or minimal importance.
But in all of them I have a function, a duty and a responsibility and I believe I will be judged on my performance of
these at the end of my time. Often I do not know exactly
what that function is—but I know that basically it is to be
a harmonizing influence, a peacemaker, a go-between, a
catalyst, a bringer-out of good qualities in others for the sake
of a group.

For me, then, the church is both a series of communities
and the means of helping me fulfill my responsibilities to
all the communities to which I belong. Unfortunately, I

have no community feeling or conscience about my parish. Its liturgy, when I used to attend the parish church, was unacceptable; its priests distant and domineering, keeping the mass to themselves, as it were, and failing (or not trying) to turn it into a community experience. The church I go to is not much better, but at least some of the priests try. I have arranged a series of house masses, to which we invite neighbors and friends but in Dublin, Ireland, this seems elitist and somehow eccentric. The children say they appreciate such masses but never initiate any move to repeat them, though I know they are very unhappy with the church liturgy.

The sacraments I see very much as community actions—the community welcoming the new member in baptism, admitting him fully in the Eucharist; initiating him further at Confirmation; witnessing his marriage; calling him to its service as a priest; shriving him of his anti-community faults, and finally commending him to God.

The church is—should be—the ideal community. It is where the love and service of our fellow-humans should be exemplified and encouraged. It is not that. I felt deeply with Charles Davis, the British theologian, who was a close friend at the time he was leaving the priesthood and the Catholic church and who complained bitterly about the lack of Christian love in it. But I still remain in the church because I feel there is something there to hold on to, something which is lying dormant and which may develop, be remolded "closer to the heart's desire." I would feel something missing if I rejected it, though I am not sure whether that is just the residue of the superstition I have tried to reject.

I make my Confession reluctantly and minimally three

or four times a year, believing that the Confession at the beginning of the mass is a more meaningful act if properly understood and performed. I receive Communion without believing fully in transubstantiation as it is presented officially, but seeing the Eucharist more in terms of transignification—an effective sign rather than as the substance of the body and blood of Christ. I believe only minimally in Papal infallibility in the accepted sense, seeing the Pope as confirming and expressing the voice of the People of God as a whole and not as speaking on his own personal account without consultation. However, I do accept that the Pope adds a final authorization to the *sensus fidelium.*

Ecumenism I deeply and fervently believe in, seeing Christian unity not just as a good thing to practice but as the most binding of God's commandments. I cannot see how we can claim to be Christian if we are not actively and urgently pursuing unity with other Christians. "Love one another" is to me the most imperative of Christ's demands and clearly directed toward our fellow Christians.

"Official" religion for me is, therefore, largely a depressing and dissatisfying facade behind which I conceal my real views, not because I have to but because, in my particular circumstances, I see no way to express them. I do not take too seriously the "orthodox Irish" view, but I have not the time nor the ability to develop in me or around me the sort of religious understanding and practices I believe in and in which I would wish to participate.

But all is not gloomy. I am Teilhardian enough to believe in the perfectibility of man. I see men as developing into God, merging into him as the soapsuds, blown through the toy pipe, merge into the bubble. In a sense, I do not see

God or man as separate but as part of a common being; man the potential realizing himself and developing into "Godness." I have a strong sense of duty, seeing my work and my family responsibilities as the service of God in and through my fellow man. To that extent, work which is personally unsatisfying—largely administration and supervising—becomes acceptable and to a degree worthwhile. I value my good relationship with my wife and, in varying degrees, with my four children. I have few very close friends and find I do not need as many acquaintances as others do though I see in those who cross my path one of the communities I serve.

Set prayer I generally avoid, though I often meditate long and deeply on the *Our Father*, trying to make its sentiments an ongoing part of my life. Mass in small groups and in informal settings I find a satisfying experience and I remember the journalists' masses and subsequent common dinners in Rome during Vatican II as the most important spiritual exercise of my life, since they naturally flowed from one another, the mass becoming the unifying bond and the meal a real *agape*. Indeed, I often find that a meal among friends is the most satisfying and meaningful form of Eucharistic experience and I am convinced that the day will soon come when the priesthood of the laity will be formally recognized. I see selected laymen being allowed—and encouraged—to preside over Eucharistic celebrations in their homes, their celebrations being overseen (episopos, or bishop, is a derivation from a Greek word meaning to "oversee") by bishops who would be as numerous as parish priests are now and dealing with only the numbers of people they could get to know personally and individually.

But I am not optimistic about the future of the Roman Catholic church from an institutional and organizational point of view. There was a time when I dismissed as peculiarly elitist the theories of Rahner and Schillebeeckx, leading European theologians, that the Roman Catholic church was going into a diaspora situation, that is, it was declining in numbers to a point where only a few hundred Catholics would remain in different countries, linked precariously with Rome. Now I think that they are probably right and that it is probably necessary if the church is to rid itself of its pomp and ceremony and its overinstitutionalized structure.

Meantime, I will keep within the structure, hoping that it will change, believing I can identify some of the changes it should adopt but not having the time, the energy or perhaps the will to help bring about the changes. I wonder how many there are who feel the same.

DESPITE FRUSTRATION, PURIFICATION

Professor of Political Science Emeritus (University of Chicago), JEROME KERWIN has long been active in Catholic lay organizations and is a past director of the Thomas More Association. Among his books are Catholic Viewpoint on Church and State *and* Government, Politics and Catholics. *He has contributed to* Commonweal *and* America *and his book reviews frequently appear in* The Critic. *A former professor at the University of Santa Clara, Mr. Kerwin now lives in Santa Clara, California.*

by Jerome Kerwin

I WRITE AS A SEPTUAGENARIAN WITH A LINGERING DOUBT whether a person of such ripe years can in any sense be considered *on the run*. At such an age does not a person stand still and watch events move rapidly by? He stands in danger of watching events with a kind of humorous scepticism that assures him he has seen all this before, or he comes to the pessimistic conclusion that things have never been worse. He must observe a balance between these extremes. If he has been an advocate in past years of drastic change in the church, he must recognize that a revolution is upon.us and that revolutions are uncontrollable; some of the things he hoped for are now realized, some things have occurred which he deplores.

If, for instance, he was a liturgist in former years he looked for the mass celebrated in his own tongue and in dignified simplicity. He never expected the strumming guitars and twanging banjos, the ear-splitting noise of traps and drums to replace the music of the majestic organ. He looked forward to the recovery of some of the solemn hymns from the Protestant hymnal, but never to music that emphasized beat rather than melody or to hymns even more sugary than the Catholic hymns of yesteryear. The young, it seems, want noise. Perhaps on reaching middle age with impaired hearing they may be satisfied with a more restrained service unto the Lord. Such is the nature of revolution that change does not come in orderly fashion. To determine my own attitude at the present time, I must look back over the past and the recent history of the church— the recent history through which I have lived.

Greek philosophers asked themselves what was the element in life that man could be most certain of, and their answer was change. Some stopped at this point, but others asked about the direction of change and arrived at a more profound philosophy. In all of life changes become necessary for men and institutions. In every situation it is either more comfortable or more profitable for some to remain as they are, but to resist an ordered review of the old invites revolution, peaceful or otherwise.

Both men and institutions may resist necessary reform for a time—the stronger the resistance the more drastic the change. Usually the revolutionary movement follows the Hegelian triad of thesis, antithesis, and synthesis, or the radical change to new ideas and institutions, the inevitable resistance and the establishment for a time of their opposite, and a final settling down to a reconciliation of the new and the old. No institution, even a divinely founded church, escapes these movements in time. Catholics have been so educated that the church has appeared as the one institution beyond change in structure and doctrine; they have lost sight of the changes that have marked the history of the church through the centuries. It has been our misfortune that the idea of the church as "the milk-white hind immortal and unchanged" has characterized official policies for too many recent generations.

What lies behind this static idea of the church? No profound view of history explains this condition. For a period of over four hundred years the church has been a beleaguered fortress. While the Reformation might have had beneficial results for all of Christendom, its general effects were calamitous. While realizing that several concurrent movements affected the religious revolt—such as the economic changes in European life, the discovery of the New World, the secularization of life through the Renaissance, dynastic rivalries, and the growing force of nationalism— one must sadly recall the lack of intelligent papal direction from Rome. Roman officialdom could not have been blind to the evils in the church or deaf to recurrent cries for reform of the ecclesiastical establishment in head and members. Leo X, busy with the accumulation of great works of art and the building of St. Peter's, could only see in the Lutheran upsurge "a monkish quarrel." Reform was too long neglected until the possibilities of reconciliation no longer existed. A delayed and necessary reformation degenerated into bitter political strife and to such bloodletting as the world had seldom seen. Rome girded itself for battle, and the Council of Trent provided the charter for the new era. A fractured Christianity settled down to years of fratricidal strife in the name of the God of peace. In the name of religion, emperors, kings, and princes rode forth to put down and slaughter fellow-Christians. The world at large turned to the more peaceful ends of secular pursuits. In the interests of survival Rome itself joined in the fray on the field of battle. It played the same game of merry Machiavel-

lian politics as all the rest. It would have required a world-
wide deluge to cleanse both the church and its Protestant
opponents of their sins.

Religious revolt led to religious anarchy; whatever elements of good—and they were not lacking—remained in
the divided parts of a once united church. The reforms demanded by the early reformers and even many within the
church appear, as one looks back upon them, reasonably
negotiable. To note a few—celibacy of the clergy, the vernacular in the liturgy, a recognition of the importance of
the laity, wider use of the scriptures, a thorough houseclean-
ing to rid the church of corruption, the nature of faith, penance and its practice, the exaggerated use of indulgences.
What a boon to all Christendom if these could have been
considered in a council in the early days of the reform movement before bitterness made discussion impossible! Are we
experiencing at the present time a reformed reformation? Is
the ecumenical movement revealing common truths long
concealed or misunderstood over the centuries? The process
of discovery and formulation is indeed slow. Yet from it
may come not one church unified in structure, but a federa-
tion of Christian churches agreed upon fundamentals and
holding in respect the differences that remain. This in no
way need diminish the Catholic's belief in the primacy of
his own church. At the same time Catholics may come to
realize that no good is accomplished by the boast, however
true, that we possess the whole truth and all others possess
but a fraction of the truth. Not even Catholics have all the
answers. Perhaps the time may come when there will be a
common recognition of the primacy of the pope when he
speaks in fatherly tones of advice rather than terrifying
tones of command.

For a Catholic to understand more fully what is now going on, it is well for him to view changing events as the reconstruction of Christianity after four centuries of internal conflict. As a result of that conflict the Catholic church remained aloof from the rest of the Christian world and often hostile to it. It tightened its grip upon its adherents, binding them in a system of laws and regulations that only an established elite could interpret.

When it retreated into its fortress the masses of people were unlettered and unlearned. They were the children of the church. Little was left for them to interpret by their own consciences. To their priests they became accustomed to turn for their religious and moral guidance. In a situation of this kind autonomy of the individual lost much of its importance, and the opportunity for the development of religious maturity was greatly diminished. For the better educated reliance upon legalistic rules resulted in a host of fine-spun interpretations. (Catholics might well be puzzled by the Friday abstinence laws that permitted Spaniards to eat meat on Fridays, but denied the privilege to other Catholics—a special dispensation given to the Spanish as a reward for their victory over the Turks at the battle of Lepanto.) The more the law was interpreted the more complicated became the law. The law was interpreted by local chancery offices, and to petitioners, chancellors, either through conscience, necessity, habit or safety, generally said, No—or some equivalent thereof. Obviously, the danger in extreme legalism is a pharisaical religious life deadening to the spirit.

The fortress mentality had significant effects upon Catholicism in the United States. From the time of the first American bishop, John Carroll, effects were made toward adjusting to a new social and political system. Bishop Carroll favored the mass in English and something similar to a trustee system in parishes. Immigration, however, forced new arrivals into congested urban ghettos, which set the church apart from the surrounding communities. Yet the church developed from these groups powerful leaders who were conscious of the advantages offered by America, and who were in no sense averse to promoting a church policy which, while truly Catholic, was nevertheless American in its attitudes and in many of its practices. While other names could be mentioned among such leaders, the names of Gibbons, Ireland, and Spaulding stand out.

Rome had neither sympathy for nor understanding of the political and social system in the United States. Rome's answer to patriotic American Catholics was that their system could in no way be considered the best since the primacy of the Catholic faith was not formally recognized, and since, if Catholics ever attained majority status, all other religions by law could at best only be tolerated. A fear in Rome that the church in America might develop too independent or too nationalistic a spirit brought a condemnation of "Americanism" and a tightening of ecclesiastical control from Rome. Despite the opposition of members of the American hierarchy an Apostolic delegate, as Rome's eyes and ears, was established in Washington. From here emanated approval of nominations to the hierarchy prior to final appointment by Rome. Clergy noted for their independence could be sure that they would never rise to the episcopal dignity. A safe and sane hierarchy was guaranteed.

The church produced the builder, the brick-and-mortar bishop, and hosts of local pastors of the same breed, although by some mistake or mysterious stroke of fate exceptions were found. Bishops and pastors untrained for such work became managers of building enterprises and deeply engaged in the world of finance. While incompetency often abounded in the system, the laity remained in the dark, for seldom was an accounting given. The bishops built extensively and sometimes lavishly, to the astonishment and envy of visiting clergy from abroad. And the church was strictly Catholic. No hierarchy in the world observed with greater obedience the orders of the Curia. All rules were strictly enforced, and the church lived aloof as a society apart from the mainstream of American life.

Great care was taken that no part of Protestantism entered American Catholic ranks. Little or no contact existed between Catholic and non-Catholic clergymen. Priests spent their lives in Catholic schools, in Catholic communities, in seminaries, and finally in their parishes. Catholic parents were warned on pain of mortal sin and denial of the sacraments not to send their children to secular schools. When in one large city the opening of a new hospital was celebrated with a civic banquet, the Catholic bishop refused to attend on the ground that clergy of other faiths would sit in equal rank with him at the speakers' table. When the Eucharistic Congress of 1926 was held in Chicago, clergymen of most religious groups generously extended their welcome to the visitors. Yet when a few years later the World Council of Churches met in Evanston, the Catholic clergy extended no such welcome, and the archbishop of Chicago answered an invitation to attend with a chilly response to the effect that Catholics were not searching for the truth, but already had it. Frequently the advances of Protestants to

Catholics met with brutal and impolite responses. Out of such a sour soil grew the rank weeds of bigotry. It flourished in both camps.

Despite an unusual growth of Catholic schools and colleges, the Catholic community produced few scholars. The Catholic professional schools produced a good crop of lawyers, doctors, and businessmen, but the field of pure scholarship languished. In the field of social action the number of Catholics involved was shamefully small. There was always a ready response to a crusade against pornographic movies; on the other hand the number of Catholics involved in the activities of the political machines in the large cities gave many good citizens the impression that Catholics operated under a dual system of morality—one public and one private.

With all this noted, however, one could not deny that church attendance and reception of the sacraments in the U.S. were surpassed by few other countries. The financial support of religious activities, involving great sacrifice on the part of many, was unexcelled. The church engaged in numerous works of charity among the poor, the sick, and the orphaned. The weakness in the system consisted largely in too great a dependence on clerical leadership and an unquestioning acceptance of directions from above. The laity marched obedient to orders from above, and critics generally came under the classification of bad or unfaithful Catholics who were disrespectful of "the mind of the church." Many Catholics failed to recognize that they were worshiping an institution in which, despite its divine founding, the human agents had been given no dispensation from the moral law.

In the face of all this where do I stand today? I have lived my life as a maverick, a person restive under the constant realization that fundamental change in the life of the church was of the greatest necessity. That life was lived in two worlds: in my education and profession it was lived in the non-Catholic world; my personal and social life was lived in the Catholic world. I knew the strength and weakness of each. I also knew the depth of bigotry in each and suffered from each. My prayers and hopes were that one day understanding would replace the bitterness of bigotry and ignorance. My belief was that if Christianity or even the Judaeo-Christian heritage was to survive at all against the growing forces of disbelief and unbelief, charity and mutual respect would have to overcome the mentality of siege and battle.

Despite some of the failures of the ecumenical movement we are entering upon the beginnings of an era of understanding and fraternal cooperation. For Catholics the era of change is often confusing and frustrating. The frustration has lost us many good souls and unfortunately will lose us more. And the road ahead may be long and tortuous. In an era of revolutionary ferment we chafe—and rightly so—at solemn official conferences over whether children should confess before first communion, or whether the laity should receive communion on the tongue or in the hand. We are justly annoyed when we read that great care must be taken that "Catholics will not have their faith disturbed by any changes." How long must the laity be treated like mindless children!

On the other hand, greater problems find their way into discussion among responsible Catholics, lay and clerical—such questions as celibacy, marriage and divorce, infallibility, the limits of authority, a new approach to the sacrament of penance—now so commonly disregarded in the older confessional form—the position of women, and the church in the social order. Anyone who can recall the spirit of only a few years ago must realize that frank and open discussion has replaced the whispered dialogue of other days. We live in a time of both challenge and frustration. The danger exists that the depressing effects of the latter will blind us to the demands of the former. Whatever the discouragement resulting from a lack of courageous and intelligent episcopal leadership, especially in the United States, a new spirit of responsible freedom is abroad in the church. Fewer Catholics attend mass with regularity, but sincere believers burdened with so many obligations "under pain of mortal sin" feel that free willing service to God should be the rule of Christian living. The church, of course, must set the general lines of faith according to the mission entrusted to her by Christ, but have there not been too many commands in the past which did not take into account the necessity for self-judgment and development of an intelligent religious maturity?

If this is an age of frustration, it may also be an age of purification. Out of it will come a church renewed. Central to Catholic thought and practice will be not individual piety, but concern for the welfare of others—already happily emphasized in the new liturgy. Some will find an era of challenge too much to bear. Many of the old props that gave us assurance have fallen into disuse. The props are gone, but the church remains. We must now depend more fully on a mature faith, not in any sense on a proud self-assurance, but on a faith seasoned by humility and sustained by God's love and understanding for erring mortals.

AVOIDING VANITY FAIR

ROSEMARY HAUGHTON is a lecturer, teacher and author of some thirty books, including The Transformation of Man *and* The Theology of Experience. *Her articles have appeared in secular and religious publications, both here and in England. Ms. Haughton and her family recently launched an experiment in Christian community living on a nine acre farm in Scotland.*

by Rosemary Haughton

I KNOW I WAS LUCKY. THE INSTRUCTION GIVEN TO MOST
converts to the church seems to consist of explanations of
the articles of Catholic faith and not much more. Like
"cradle" Catholics, they are not expected to need more in
the way of spiritual guidance than exhortations to go to the
sacraments regularly and say the rosary, and perhaps a
"morning offering."

For me it was different. Possibly because I was very young
(barely sixteen) I was under instruction for about nine
months. Also I got my teaching not from an overworked
pastor in half-hours pried out of a too-full day, but from a
Benedictine nun of a community which made the instruction of converts its special work. So there was a feeling of
leisure, both ways.

I did get the doctrine—in a fat black book with two sizes
of print (large for "essentials" and small for explanations)
and lots of footnotes. It was a terrible little book, the kind
that is always denounced nowadays, but in my enthusiasm I
read it like a thriller—on the bus, on the beach, and in my
bath. I also devoured Catholic novels about the persecutions
under Queen Elizabeth I, and (after all, I *was* only sixteen)

Catholic novels for children. And lives of saints, of course.
But—and this is much more surprising—my instructress, a
tiny frail old nun with soft but shrewd brown eyes, dropped
me in at the deep end of Catholic spirituality. She gave me
(among the didactic novels and the lives of saints and the
catechism), the works of Abbot Marmion, the letters of
Dom Chapman and of Janet Erskine Stuart, de Caussade's
"Abandonment to Divine Providence" and Saint Francis de
Sales' "Treatise on the Love of God."

I understood about half, and it must be admitted that I
sometimes turned with relief to the pious novels; but I did
learn one thing that a great many Catholics seem never to
have realized, to their eventual undoing. I perceived, in a
muddly "teenage way," that the main thing about being a
Catholic was loving God and knowing him in prayer, and
that the service of others grew out of *that*. The doctrine part
I seized on hungrily, for I found the intellectual challenge
exciting and stimulating, and I argued with my patient instructress over difficult bits, in a brash "teenage style."
But the little old lady was endlessly patient and quite un-
shockable. It was the "spiritual" part that remained with
me. Independently, after my reception, I read St. John of
the Cross and Julian of Norwich, rather than theology.

Many years later, when theology was much more to me
than something for an underexercised mind to chew on, I
was still never tempted to substitute theology for spirituality. So when the upheavals came I had something to pull
me through.

As I said, I was lucky. Not only did I encounter some of
the masters of Christian spirituality right from the beginning but my very ignorance prevented me from assuming,

as many Catholics do, that to "cultivate" any but vocal prayer is a presumptuous attempt to gate-crash a party of the spiritual elite. On the contrary, it was impressed on me by one writer after another that to desire a deep and conscious awareness of God, and get it, was *normal* for a Christian.

Normal, however, isn't the same as average. The Christian norm is Christ, which seems to make the phrase meaningless, because he is unique. But if he is "the first-born among many brethren," the eldest brother's experience is obviously important, and oneness of mind and heart with the Father was his leading characteristic. This oneness the spiritual writers called "contemplative prayer," though they varied in descriptions of how best to get it, and what were the symptoms of having got it. (It has this resemblance to the common cold, that you can't get it by deciding to, but if you do the things that bring it on, you get it!)

The discovery that there exists a way of *knowing God* while still earth-fast is an overwhelming bit of information. If you are, as I was, young and enthusiastic and extremely ignorant you make some mistakes. I made all the classic mistakes (you can find them in the manuals of the spiritual life if you care to look) and a few extra ones, such as trying to force my early married and domestic life into a kind of pseudomonastic mold. It didn't work, mercifully, but I, and my suffering family, learned some useful things in the process, like hospitality as a way of life instead of a social custom, and the fact (forgotten too easily) that a big group of people can do, and bear, things that break up a small one. We discovered this by being (eventually) a family of ten. With constant additions of official and unofficial "foster-children" life developed a momentum of its own. There was no need to instill virtues with long explanations or exhortations, because their practical usefulness was obvious, as were the immediately noticeable results of the lack of them, in quarrelsomeness, restless discontent, jealousy, and silliness all round. (St. Paul said it all a long time ago, but it has to be rediscovered each time.)

But if you have a huge family, a succession of extra (problem) children, and a necessarily big home with no money for domestic help, and if on top of that you write and lecture to help pay for it all (my husband being a school master) when and how—if at all—do you pray? And, in a sense, why? Surely doing all that is *enough?* God can't ask the impossible.

The short answer is that it's impossible if you *don't* pray, as I discovered, because for a long time I didn't. I suppose it can be done by superwomen with unlimited energy and inventiveness, but I wonder—perhaps to console myself— whether the superwomen make the best job of dealing with *people*, as opposed to routines? But for non-superwomen like myself the nonstop work, bouts of illness, anxiety, recurrent financial crises, as well as all the usual problems of bringing up a family: All this very easily leads either to a dogged sticking-to-the-routine mentality which leaves no room for love or fun or imagination, or else to nervous irritability, or both. With me it was the latter, and those early days when I pictured myself as the Ideal Catholic Mother "praying as I worked" and surrounded by infants enjoying domestic liturgies (learned from books) gave way to a dismal, obstinate clinging on to shreds of idealism and hope. I must have been a very trying mother, during the years when I felt faith sliding away from me, further and further, the more I clutched. I longed for someone to prop me up, but there was nobody. I had to do the propping, for people who assumed that I could give them what they needed, and I suppose it was a good thing—I just had to put a good face on it and carry on.

There were too many babies, also, one after another, and altogether too much work, and a kind of despair gradually gripped me, so that one day I sat on the edge of my bed at dawn and realized why people can commit suicide in spite of loving their families.

I don't know whether it is being partly Jewish, but there is something *in* me (it seems to operate independently of my feelings and thoughts) that won't quite give up. Whenever I thought I'd hit bottom, emotionally and morally and spiritually, something yanked me up just enough to carry on. I didn't pray—I told myself I couldn't—but one lifeline at least was the custom of family prayers with the children, ridiculous and exhausting and futile as it often seemed. I'd started that long before, and I couldn't face their questions and bewilderment if I stopped. So I went on, and I had to go through the motions, say things, explain things, think of ideas for readings, celebrations. Sometimes it was agonizing and I felt a hypocrite, but it was (though I'd forgotten that for a time) what those old books ordered: keep going, go through the motions, never give up. Besides this, the family had this momentum of its own, of hospitality and "practical Christianity," and whereas I had, in earlier years, striven to create this, now it carried me.

Later, things got worse, for there was added to my private stresses the public ones of the post-Vatican II traumas. So,

when the doubt and storms of the theological free-for-all
were at their worst, and people were abandoning the church
right and left with colossal self-righteousness, my own
private life was already in the kind of moral and emotional
mess that makes any faith seem empty and impossible. The
two things together bereft me of any reason that I could see
for going on calling myself a Christian.

There was no one to help me. (There often isn't. The
nice idea that wise old spiritual directors are always supplied
by the Lord in moments of crisis is, alas, not true.) By this
time, in fact, things were far worse than before, for the
curious reason that there had been a period of intense
"light." It happened when I had been nursing a mentally
sick cousin and had reached a point of almost mindless ex-
haustion. One day I awoke to a world transformed into a
paradise of effortless joy and prayer, combined with renewed
and apparently inexhaustible physical energy. It lasted several months, and among other things (as is to be expected
and desired), it released in me a morality that sprang from
inner freedom and love, replacing the previous one which I
recognized as "conditioned," though right and valuable. But I
had forgotten the emphatic teaching of the great masters. I
didn't use that time of joy firmly and constructively, and
when it faded I faded too. So the newly epidemic doubts,
plus personal emotional problems, found me undefended
even by the strong bastions of an accepted code. It was then
that I showed (though I did not know it at the time) the
terrible truth of the saying of Jesus, "If the light that is in
you be darkness, how great is that darkness!"

But it was then, at that time of utter blackness, that some
of the teaching of those half-understood and almost forgotten books came back to me. Why should I pretend? I

asked myself. I shan't be the first or the last who has discovered that Christianity, however beautiful, is not real after all. I've struggled and tried and carried on, and it has let me down. But another voice, instructed by those great masters, replied firmly, "If there *is* any truth in all that you have believed, you won't rediscover it by cutting the wires." This made sense, even then, so I carried on going to mass and teaching the children, and it was more depressing than ever. It was even harder to maintain the difficult balancing act involved in writing as a Catholic, for Catholics, without committing myself to beliefs in which I could see little meaning.

It worked. They had said it would, and it did. In the end I came out of the tunnel into a light far brighter than any I had known before. It happened because someone I knew, at a certain moment, told me: "Pray! If you can do no more —yell at God, scream at him in anger and pain—but pray!" And I did, and the darkness fled as it fled on Easter morning.

The tragedy is that so few people have encountered the height and depth and richness of Catholic spirituality, from the Desert Fathers to Thomas Merton. Often enough, when modern Catholics feel a need for a deeper, more vivid spiritual experience they look for it in the East, and import Hindu or Buddhist spirituality, or adaptations of them, into their Catholicism, or emigrate spiritually, leaving the church behind. Frequently they don't even know that there *is* a Western mystical tradition. But the Eastern mystical tradition grows out of a culture totally different from ours, and on the whole if it is imported it must be distorted to fit an alien way of thought. The alternative really is a divorce from Western culture, which is no bad thing in itself, yet the West cannot simply be written off as spiritually damned.

The Western Christian has a mission to his own people, and he will find the means to their (and his) enlightenment on his doorstep. At a later stage of spiritual growth the two traditions may meet, and help each other, as they clearly did for Thomas Merton, but they are deeply distinct, culturally and historically. And the ancient Western spirituality is rich, strong, vivid and much more "whole" and earthy than the Eastern.

So at least I have found it. I had proved the teaching true, the hard way, though it was some years before I could bring myself to believe that I could not only stay out of that pit but recover (with a far more mature understanding) the reality of the spiritual search. Eventually another Christian, a nun whose deep and spontaneous humility never let her notice what she was doing, pushed me "over the edge" and I found the simplest prayer, the one that is really the only possible kind for people who must be always on the run: —that odd, unpredictable "unknowing" of contemplation.

So in the end I knew that you have to *stop* running, you have to be still. And you know, then, that a lot of the running is futile and unnecessary and even evil. It seems hard for our busy culture to believe, but once you stop, and fall for a while into that peace, you begin to hear when God says "run" and when it's the devil giving you a shove. So you run when God tells you, and other times you try to sit still with God, at least (like St. Catherine who did it really efficiently) in the place within that God gradually makes for himself even in the busiest life, if you let him.

Then it ceases to matter so much that you are vain and lazy and irritable, that you care too much for what others think, and mistake your own will for God's. He'll take care of that, in time, if you let him.

Once you have let yourself drop over the edge into that "unknowing," feelings and moods matter less. Sometimes you want to turn back, it looks too deep and huge down there, but there are the great teachers to tell you the fall is really *upwards*.

Another thing they tell you is the need for vocal prayer. The novice may be tempted to despise it; the master knows it matters to *say* things. East or West, you need a "mantra," a verbal "way in." Around the inner temple there is that "forecourt" of prayer which matters so much because it is always there even when, for a time, the door of the inner temple seems shut. It can be, most beautifully, the ancient prayer of the church, the "opus Dei" of the monks, modified now (and in temporary blue plastic covers) and yet still keeping its roots in the deep past, the Christian past and the Hebrew heritage of ever-astonishing psalms.

Divine office? At home? It could mean less T.V., getting up a bit earlier, going to bed twenty minutes later. How impossible! But we do these things willingly to keep an important appointment, or go to a party. And it isn't impossible once you stop running. The Divine Office is not everyone's garden of delights, but there is also the rosary, or it could be as well, in odd moments of quiet, when sleepiness or harassment makes the quietness difficult. And the "new" techniques are very, very good, too, for those who try them, but they all lead the same way.

There is time, there has to be time, or the running will take us right out of God's country into the wild hopelessness of the limbo of Vanity Fair, which is full of good, kind, busy people who haven't seen God's red light, his "stop" sign.

"Be still, and know that I am God." It's sanity, light, free-

dom. It's also pain and longing and a restless desire which
is never satisfied, a truthful consciousness of the sin that
divides us from the perfect peace, and a knowledge of all the
sadness and badness in ourselves and others that demands
both repentance and concern, and so seldom gets them. So
it's not, as many imagine, a comfortable warm bath of the
spirit, a refuge from the trials of this mortal life. It is a discovery at the very heart of life.

It's really there, that "cloud of unknowing" which is
God's dwelling. It is home, it is Self, it is the one thing
necessary. It waits, on nights when the baby has just gone
back to sleep after a 2 A.M. feeding, on mornings hanging
out the wash, or tidying a child's bedroom, on afternoons in
the middle of a crowded store, or when the shadows under
the trees talk about the continuity of growth and earth and
the rolling seasons. It is there after evenings of play and
reading aloud with the children, or later, plowing with
them through the problems of an adolescent love affair. It
doesn't make things easier, in fact in a way it makes them
harder because it cuts out self-pity and refuses the refuge of
resentment and revenge. But it does make life *alive*, with
some sense of priorities, of hope, of meaning. A lot of things
that used to matter no longer matter, in the light of that
dark knowing. Imperceptibly, they've just dropped away.
One is lighter, freer.

At forty-six, with four adult children and two more nearly
so (only four at home for a while yet), there's a new life to
make, maybe at last there's real work for God, work I can do
because I have, finally, learned to stop running for the sake
of running. I could have learned this years ago if I'd paid
attention to the masters, but I was too arrogant, too confi-

dent, too selfish. I thought I knew it all, and had to find out that my own knowledge was deadly and destructive. Now that I've stopped running I can really begin. I wonder what is round the next corner? And the *last* corner? That is the most important question, but then, in a way, I know the answer. It will mean really letting go, with nothing to hold on to any more, and falling, falling—upwards.

COLOR IT BLACK

Being under fifty, KIERAN QUINN did not actually live in biblical times. But the scores of cartoons he has published on religious and scriptural themes have provoked reactions which make him feel an intense kinship with Daniel in the Lion's Den. A native of Cincinnati, where he studied art and has had five one-man shows, Mr. Quinn teaches painting and works as a freelance artist. His cartoons have been anthologized and reprinted in several books and magazines.

by Kieran Quinn

HIS SERMONS ALWAYS BEGAN THE SAME WAY. "DEARLY beloved brethren in Christ Jesus our Lord." And throughout the half-hour discourse there were a dozen more "dearly beloved's" and then, toward the end, a series of "and in conclusion, dearly beloved brethren in Christ Jesus our Lord." The first "in conclusion" heralded only the beginning of the end. At least ten minutes to go.

I was one of his altar boys. He was the monsignor, a tall, gaunt ascetic man with piercing eyes, black cape, biretta, breviary invariably in hand with its gold edges turning black and dollar bills stuck in it as place markers. I once saw a twenty dollar bill. Occasionally he played golf, rarely enjoyed a cigar but I never saw him in secular dress. Alcoholic beverages, even beer, were never allowed in the rectory. He was the epitome of the detached, spiritual man, the most otherworldly of creatures. He was the Right Reverend Monsignor James Spalding Elder, pastor irremoveable of St. Rose parish, Lima, Ohio.

He had a kind face and smile, spoke softly but when the occasion required could be stern and demanding. Once, as I was preparing charcoal for benediction, he came up to me and said, "Charles, come here." We walked to a corner of the sacristy and he gestured gracefully with his exquisitely fashioned hand at a lonely, burnt matchstick there on an otherwise immaculate floor. "Charles," he said, slowly, solemnly, pausing after each word, "Charles . . . this . . . is . . . the . . . house . . . of . . . God." I picked up the match. It seemed to me then that God himself could not have been more impressive. I am not kidding. Anyway, I got my first lesson in spirituality from him. I concluded that the truly spiritual man dressed in black, wore a cape, carried a breviary, was oblivious to creature comforts, called people "dearly beloved" and drove an old Buick. Was there any doubt?

So I went to the minor seminary. The world could use another Monsignor Elder. But my views on spirituality had to be modified a bit. You see I entered a Franciscan seminary and the friars dress in brown, not black. Can I ever forget my first meeting with a real, genuine friar? I had corresponded with the man many times. Now it was time for a face to face confrontation. Suddenly, from down the long, gleaming, terrazo corridor there was a peculiar sound like the funeral beat of a muffled drum. Later on I realized that the sound was caused by a heavy rosary suspended from a rope around the man's waist, banging against an obviously very bony knee. The specter came closer. I could make out in the dimly lit hall a long, flowing, brown robe draped on a living skeleton. My God, he was more spiritual looking than Monsignor Elder. Could that be possible? The Reverend Ermin Schneider of the Order of Friars Minor of the Province of St. John the Baptist, Cincinnati, Ohio was positively emaciated, a Peter of Alcantara incarnate. Now I knew for certain that the spiritual man dressed in brown, wore a white rope, a heavy rosary that made noise, a brown cape and had a deep, magnificently resonant voice. He was also terribly skinny and, like Monsignor Elder, occasionally smoked cigars.

On a warm, August morning, unworthy as I was even after my first eight-day retreat, I was invested in the heavy, itchy, brown serge habit; the white rope with three knots, one for poverty, one for chastity, one for obedience; a rosary that didn't bang very loudly either because the beads were too small or my knee too fat; and finally a pair of sandals that at first hurt my feet. From the steps of the sanctuary I was given a new name, a new identity. "From now on Charles Quinn will be known in religious life as Friar Kieran." The ecstasy of it all. I was on my way. I recall feeling sorrow for those left behind in the world who, since they were not called like me, could not pursue whole-heartedly the spiritual life nor scale the heights—who could never become like Monsignor Elder or Father Ermin. Pity.

For the next nine years I was indoctrinated in an elab-orate apparatus which would transform me from a fun-loving kid into a serious, spiritual adult. There was much to learn and much to practice. Permit me to list a few of the things over which we agonized. There was the mystery of meditation, its techniques and methods. And for spiritual reading shall it be Marmion or the revelations of Mary of Agrega? Then, what is the difference between a particular and general examination of conscience? What is my dom-inant fault? That required the most work. Divine office was always a problem. Those damn psalms. They are bad enough in English. We had to struggle with them in Latin.

Besides all this, weekly confession, the crown rosary, holy
hours, table prayers and reading, rules of discipline, rule
of St. Francis, general constitutions of the order, statutes of
the province.

Now understand, we were not seeking merely Christian
spirituality but a brand of it called Franciscan, which makes
quite a difference. Let me give you an example. We were
encouraged to foster interest in the liturgy, but not too
much interest. That savored of monasticism. And our meditations ought not to be too cerebral. That was Dominican.

Throughout my seminary days and on past my ordination
I did not doubt the Monsignor Elder ideal of spirituality. I
had no reason to. In fact I didn't doubt anything. We were
trained to accept the authority of others, either the teaching
of the church or the opinions of recognized theologians.
To think for oneself was dangerous. But after a few years
in the priesthood I began to think for myself, at first cau-
tiously, hesitantly. I was reading extensively the new theology and psychology in books and magazines. The Catholic
world was in intellectual ferment. Clerical defections were
increasing and they were not all obvious misfits. I recall the
impact I felt when Charles Davis left. Theologians were
becoming bolder. The whole atmosphere was changing
from one of comfortable certitude to disquieting questioning. I began to test the traditional Christian teaching
against the way I experienced life. I began to form my own
opinions. I was thrilled when I discovered in authors like
Leslie Dewart or John McKenzie a confirmation of my own
awkward and amateurish theologizing.

For years the most baffling issue of all for me, one with
extensive ramifications, was the insoluble dichotomy I saw

in Christianity between the spiritual and secular spheres. It appeared to me that the believer was caught in a schizoid existence, a double life, membership in two worlds, a secular and a religious one. I could see evidence all around me of this spiritual schizophrenia, not only in myself but in the lives of my associates and friends. The typical Sunday Catholic is the best example.

Strangely, I felt that it was this emphasis upon a spiritual world which made possible a secular kind of existence, which divorced religion from daily life. In a way it was causing the problem it was trying to solve. I began to ask whether or not a spiritual world existed. Perhaps the supernatural was a myth. In other words when the Christian preacher insists upon the necessity of love and the psychologist says the same thing are they talking about the identical truth? I concluded that the automatic reception of the sacraments, the perfunctory liturgy with its rites and ceremonies did not effectively manipulate a supernatural world of grace. That world did not exist. To me Christianity has meaning only insofar as it casts light upon my experience of life. I think it does that.

The institution of religious life came in for prolonged scrutiny. After considerable study, it seemed to me that the gospel counsels of poverty, chastity and obedience had questionable scriptural support. As one scholar put it, they are neither evangelical nor are they counsels. In other words, there is no reason to believe that the gospel presents a twofold Christian life, one mediocre, the other perfect. Besides, the institution of religious life as we know it today derives from monasticism which required a flight from the world, placing oneself at a distance from it, dividing the day into

distinct periods of prayer and work, thereby achieving perfection.

We tend to forget, I think, the pervasive influence of
monasticism in the life of the church even to the present
day, in the formation of the clergy, both diocesan and
regular. An average Sunday sermon will invariably betray
that influence. One can readily admit the enormous cultural
contribution of traditional religious life while at the same
time questioning its relevance to the gospel. One scripture
scholar says, with no little caution, that monasticism is not
the first conclusion one reaches in reading the New Testament. I am inclined to go further: Monasticism appears to
be an insidious heresy which negates the major consequence
of the incarnation, namely, that the Christian finds salvation
where he is and he is in the world. We are called to effect
the kingdom of God in the world, not to create another one.

One of the worst effects of all this was a division of the
Christian populace into religious and lay, a polarization
lamented by the late Dietrich Bonhoeffer. Religious, of
course, were in an enviable position. They had chosen the
better part by sitting at the feet of the Master. Lay people
were encouraged, insofar as possible in their less fortunate
circumstances, to emulate the life style of the religious.
They, too, could reach holiness if they followed a modified
program of monasticism, if they would interrupt daily routine and practice the spiritual exercises canonized by the
monks—the reading of scripture, formal prayer, meditation,
acts of mortification and the frequent reception of the sacraments. The more laymen would do this the better they
would become. No doubt about it.

The pursuit of spirituality, apparently, requires us to take
time out during the day and do something specifically re-

ligious, like make a retreat, attend devotions, say the rosary, go to mass, pray the psalms. Incredibly, we've sold this monumental nonsense to generations of believers. It's time to stop. Fortunately, there is a new vision of Christianity on the horizon, one that will direct the believer's energies toward understanding through faith his life in the world. The Christian of the future will not be called to create a spiritual world apart but to realize that his world is, through faith, a spiritual one. The kingdom is within. The writings of Eugene Kennedy and Gregory Baum come to mind here.

Church structure came in for a measure of mulling over. You find that institutionalized Christianity is very meaning-ful to those who have made it a full-time business, whose livelihood depends upon it. Naturally. But I am amused by the professional ecclesiastic trying to convince the world of the absolute necessity of structure, of the necessity of lit-urgy, sacraments and priestly functions which, in effect, de-fine his existence. We all like to be wanted, to be needed. It all boils down to the fact there is a great difference be-tween Christianity and institutionalized Christianity.

We give this truth too little thought. What is happening now in the north of Ireland is a good example. Obviously a betrayal of Christianity, it is nonetheless the logical conse-quence of two institutions, one Catholic and one Protes-tant, who have traditionally hated each other. So they fight. They hate each other because they were taught by their respective institutions to hate. Historically, the Christian church has been anti-Semitic. Jews were denied membership in the medieval guilds and forced to live in ghettos. And in the Good Friday liturgy we used to pray, "pro perfidis Judaeis," which used to be translated "for the perfidious Jews." It was softened up a bit to read "for the unbelieving

Jews," but in neither case is it a compliment. I grew up in St. Rose parish of Lima, Ohio, disliking Protestants and Jews—not overtly, but it was a feeling we all had. After all, they were wrong, were they not? We were right.

The institution gets in the way of Christianity as much as it helps. That is the way I read history. Structure, as we know it, is not necessary for the existence and spread of Christianity. Structure is merely convenient and useful up to a point. The early church did quite well without file cabinets. When you turn religion into a business, you need file cabinets, which are damnably fascinating things, and all of a sudden you have people intensely interested not in Christianity but in the business of Christianity. Witness corporate Catholicism today. If that is what Christ had in mind I will eat this paper. Christianity is an idea, a life style, a way of looking at the world and oneself. If it is lived it will grow and spread by the very power of that witness.

Christianity can not be defined by an organization or structure because it is essentially a movement. In a way it is supra-institutional, transcending the limits of various sects and churches all too often at each other's throats. Certainly one does not become Christian by affiliation with a Christian church. That brings us to the crucial question. What is Christianity?

One thing for sure, it has to do with God since it is a religion. That goes without saying but the problem is we ought to be saying more about it. The concept of God is almost taken for granted. One author recently complained that he was tired of listening to theologians talking about God as if they had just had lunch with him. Despite scripture and human theologizing God remains and will remain a terribly unfamiliar reality. We can never get the arms of our minds around him. It is quite true to say that when theologians discuss God they do not know what they are talking about, which is not to demean their intelligence but to assess realistically its potential. They get a better hold of truth when they try to discover what God is not.

About thirty years ago I came upon the small, blue volume by Johannes Lindworsky entitled, *The Psychology of Asceticism*. In it the author made a point which has stuck with me only to be reinforced by Dewart's books many years later. It is this: Our attitude toward religion, God, the world, the hierarchy, morality, heaven and hell are, in the last analysis, determined by what kind of idea we've formed of divinity. So when you hear people discussing or arguing religion you can bet that the difference or convergence of viewpoint hinges upon a concept of God.

I think the usual idea of God is of a superperson, with supermind and will, very powerful, who has the whole world in his hands and who can do anything. He's laid out pretty well what is right and wrong in his commandments and he takes a dim view of transgressions. But he is loving and merciful when you are sorry. He likes being acknowledged and worshiped also.

Such a view of God has ample support in the bible and, of course, would be accurate if we can take scripture literally. But can we? The above description seems far too anthropomorphic and intellectually not very satisfying. Granted that God has revealed himself as a person, can we conclude that he is a person? Not necessarily. Perhaps he chose that way as the best vehicle for revelation. And if God's work seems to proceed from a mind and will, can we conclude he has a mind and will as we know them? No. For the same reason we do not believe God has a left hand or right hand or really experiences the emotion of anger even though the bible says these things.

Perhaps, we inch closer to the truth by saying that God is neither a person or a being as we experience them but a reality who makes presence felt in beings. He is not the highest being in the hierarchy of beings, which puts him awfully far away from us, but a presence that pervades the existence of all being, is being's support and source and therefore very close to us. That presence is recognized through faith. I mean we cannot logically conclude that God exists, neither can we conclude that he does not exist. If my experience of life points to the presence of something else not immediately attainable by the senses or mind, I can make a leap of faith and believe in God. If my experience points to nothing else existing I can make an act of faith in atheism.

These considerations are admittedly tedious if not boring, but the practical consequences are staggering. For example, if God does not have a mind he doesn't make up his mind regarding right and wrong, about where the world is going, what I should do or the outcome of tomorrow's weather. Sounds great, doesn't it? But that is not the case. Right and wrong remain very real possibilities but the criterion has shifted to figuring it out for myself. That is hard. And if God does not manipulate the world according to a master plan who is in control? We are. We control not only our personal destiny but collectively the destiny of the whole world. We have the power to create a heaven or hell personally or globally. We can succeed or fail, and this is an awesome responsibility. We cannot count on a *deus ex machina* waiting in the wings.

The God we deal with is a God of revelation. Now this usually means that he has told us a definite number of truths about himself and ourselves in scripture. But for me that view is too restrictive. Rather, God continually reveals his presence as we live out our lives if we have the eyes of faith to see it. But we must note carefully the way in which he reveals himself. It is always indirectly, obliquely, in something else. My favorite quote here is from the Emmaus story. "They recognized the Lord in the breaking of the bread." Martin Buber says the same thing but in a different way. We encounter God in the sending, in the mission of life.

It seems to me that whenever there is an explosion of either truth, goodness or beauty into our lives divinity is in some way breaking through. It may be the incredible grace of a ballerina, the warm, comforting sound of a ballad, the fleeting color of a sunset, the eroticism of a nude body, the mystery of a computer, the eternal crashing surf, the sleek design of a Ferrari, the lined resignation in the face of the aged. I am sure some of us will find God more easily and more surely in a bouquet of flowers than in the monstrance of benediction, in the face of a child rather than in the routine Sunday liturgy, more in the frenzied play of ghetto children than in the somber gait of a Forty Hours procession. Picasso can reveal divinity as well as St. Paul; perhaps, too, the antics of Jonathan Winters or Moms Mabley. Why not?

Pace the pentecostals, I think the direct pursuit of God is an illusion and a fairly common one. Of course, the human animal can believe and be convinced of absolutely anything. And there are many people who think they experience and feel divinity directly. If it works, fine. But we must remember that there is very little support in the New Testament for the direct pursuit of God, only a couple of texts, at most. And yet there is a lot said there about finding God indirectly, in feeding the hungry, giving drink to the thirsty, clothing the naked. The direction of the New Testament is unmistakably horizontal, toward our neighbor, not toward God. For good reason, too. He doesn't need food, drink or clothing and our neighbor does.

The Christian discovers God in the world, in the experience of life, in personal relationships. Unlike other religions the Christian does not need a church as a place of contact with divinity. He needs a church as a place of contact with his neighbor. So the early Christians did not build churches. They met together in homes to celebrate and to affirm communally what was happening to them in the world, what they had experienced there, the presence of God and the saving grace of the Lord Jesus. They came together to celebrate what they had experienced, not in order to experience it. This is uniquely Christian. If church buildings are unimportant, so also are ecclesiastical personnel, like popes, bishops, priests, deacons, subdeacons, lectors, etc. They have a legitimate role as teachers, ministers and representatives but they are hardly as important as they would make us believe today. Christianity was not founded upon sacred persons and sacred places.

If it is true that God reveals himself, it is equally true he hides himself. Divinity is a very unobtrusive reality and whereas we have plenty of books on revelation we lack a theology of God's silence. The truth is we really don't need

God for a fulfilled human existence. Any magnificent obsession will do. He has made us independent of himself. That is his greatest gift to us. And I don't think he cools his heels waiting for recognition and gratitude.

The idea that God is fascinated by glowing candles, clouds of incense, profound bows or genuflections is an interesting one. So also the idea that we can manipulate him with ritual. There are many things God is not. He certainly is not a jealous oriental monarch or a cantankerous renaissance prince. Is there any good reason to treat him as such, other than the fact we have grown accustomed to it? Worship and prayer have a place not because they do anything to or for God but because they do something to and for us. We will live better if we stop to think about and celebrate our relationship to divinity and to realize the inexhaustible source of potential growth within us because of that relationship. I think the significant point in both prayer and worship is how much we can do for ourselves. But "religious" people are always trying to get God to do things. Well, he doesn't.

Notice, too, that the mood of our worship is depressingly solemn. We see few smiles in church and a lot of sullen faces. For that reason we associate God with extreme seriousness and serious things. The demure countenance of the celibate nun reminds us more of God than the wild orgasms of newly-weds. God seems to be far away at those very moments when we are most human, times of fun, laughter, excitement, sexual pleasure, awe, wonderment, silliness because these things are rarely part of our worship. We are victims of the Monsignor Elder syndrome of spirituality. We color it black. But how many black flowers are there?

The atmosphere of a night club with its music, fun, eating and drinking together, its conviviality and joy is closer in many respects to a genuine celebration of life than our Sunday liturgy. Things are changing, with liturgy becoming more human, but I wonder sometimes if it is not merely a veneer over a still strong and grim tradition. The concept of God must change.

If religion has a lot to do with God it has a lot to do with man. Strangely, all religions agree on one point, that we are not what we ought to be. They agree on the possibility and necessity of change. We must become other than what we are in order to find perfection. Christianity expresses this fact with its insistence on conversion, metanoia, as a condition for salvation. Traditionally, we were encouraged to save our souls. Life here on earth was merely a preparation for a far more important existence in eternity. Recently, the emphasis has changed and an attempt is being made to relate the Christian message to the here and now, where, I think, it properly belongs.

We are born. We live a while. We die. In between birth and death there is a process of growth. That is what life is all about and that is what religion is all about. To me, Christianity is an elaborate myth which reveals with consummate beauty and truth the dynamic of personal growth, the maturation of the human personality. Christianity tells me the things that will make me grow and the things that will make me die as a person. Central to the Christian message is the importance of love. In reality it is its essence. We grow and develop our potentialities in and through love relationships throughout life. We cannot turn away from self toward the pain and ecstasy of involvement except in an atmosphere of acceptance and affirmation. The rhythm of growth is one of death and resurrection, of beginning over and over again when we have been hurt or have failed. Love makes this possible. To mature, we need the support of human fellowship.

But I have no faith in sectarian community, in Catholic community, in Jewish community, in Protestant community, in Black community. Nonsense. We are a human community. We are brothers with a common relationship with divinity and a common destiny. True, there are real differences between peoples, cultural and social but although fascinating, they are superficial. Ethnic pride is understandable but in the long run becomes devisive. Christianity proclaims that we are related in our humanity and that we ought to treat each other as brothers, sharing what we are and what we have with our neighbor. Sounds very impractical and so it is. But being a Christian means showing the world what it means to be human. Just as Christ showed us what it means to be human.

It was time now to leave the priesthood and religious life. On October 20, 1967 I knocked on the door of my provincial superior, walked in and handed him a letter requesting reduction to the lay state. He glanced at the letter, looked up and said, "You're kidding." I wasn't and he knew it. So I am back again in the world. I have come full circle, ready to start again. I shall never become like Monsignor Elder or Father Ermin.

I've abandoned all the old roadmaps to holiness, discarded the elaborate prescriptions for spirituality. My main business now is living, plain and simple. And I think there is a certain kind of living that will reveal God to me. But I am not out after him. If he comes into my life it will be by the back door. My task, I see now, is one of becoming more human, not more spiritual—more compassionate, joyful, forgiving, more loving and sensitive to all forms of beauty, goodness, truth wherever I find them. I must be willing to change, to become what I am not, to leave behind what I was. I must be unafraid of life, confident of the resources within me and dare to dream impossible dreams because I live and breathe in the mysterious presence of a reality we define as Love, who is the source of all the things I want to become.

TO CELEBRATE
THE COMMONPLACE

Married and a resident of Chicago, JOHN SPRAGUE is the Promotion Director of the Thomas More Association. A former assistant editor of The Critic, *Mr. Sprague received degrees from Laval University, Quebec, and the Gregorian University in Rome.*

by John Sprague

BY WAY OF INTRODUCTION, LET ME DESCRIBE MYSELF AS AN efficiency expert, for lack of a better word. It's not my occupation; it's a drive I have—to be efficient, right, fast, on time, every time, with an answer for every question, or know where to find one, recognizing the best choices, striving to remember everything, saving things that someday will come in handy, looking for value. The perfect product of the American way. I normally keep all this to myself (though some friends imply I should keep more of it to myself), but it's the way I am.

Actually, I've got a fast-paced job that requires remembering hordes of details and keeping my patience until I'm ready to split. I never have less than a dozen projects going at once and by the time one is finished it seems I've started several more. But I have always enjoyed being involved in more than I could manage with ease in the allotted time. There's always more time somehow to get the job done.

I do get frustrated though; things don't go my way one hundred precent of the time (lately I'd even hesitate to estimate what percent). But I consider myself very lucky: I thoroughly enjoy my work. I love my wife more than anything. And I feel my future is bright, if the world doesn't come apart at the seams around me. So I keep planning ahead, trusting in the same good fortune I've enjoyed all along, and I thank God step by step.

Still, everything doesn't come up roses, and some things that I should enjoy more I can't. I enjoy my job, for instance, but I'll never be able to enjoy getting to and from work. There is something about being herded into a rush-hour subway that challenges my sanity. I'm not a cow. And facing the expressways twice a day is hardly an alternative. I enjoy many things, from sports, movies and theater to learning languages and visiting foreign countries. But I don't like the idea that there are so many things I'll never be able to do or have simply because I'll never have enough "green stuff" to afford it. Money seems to be such a poor measure of who should do or be what they could. But it's an unchangeable fact that I guess I'm stuck in the system along with everyone else.

I am more and more getting the impression that people are less and less doing things for others just for the sake of the doing, or for the satisfaction of being a friend. I enjoy doing things—little things or big—for others. They are grateful for being considered with friendship; they always show it. I think if I had to spend my life at a job that only gave me money to enjoy I'd never make it. Then I would be just one of the herd.

My biggest prayer in life right now is one of thanks— thanks for the meaningful things that fill my life. As short a time as five years ago, my basic prayer was something like, "Lord, help me find where I'm going!" I am grateful for all the developments in my life, for the direction I've taken, the decisions I've made, the people who helped me, and I like to share that feeling of gratefulness.

It's not always easy to share something as meaningful as happiness, or a feeling of thankfulness because you feel blessed in some way. And I guess I'm getting more and more cynical about prayer. Prayer has to be meaningful conversation between myself and God, or perhaps among myself, those I am with, and God. For a number of reasons I find it next to impossible to pray in church, at mass. If the parish I belong to were small, and had a small congregation where I wasn't just a face in the crowd, it might be different, though I'm not sure. There is too little conversation where I worship and too much spectatorship. The impersonality, routineness, lack of enthusiasm and overprogramming turn me off.

I don't know what can be done about the church in general (and I hesitate to speak of "the church" because I feel I am very much part of the church, for one thing, and I have a good number of friends, exclassmates, priests, who would take exception to some of the things I say). I'm not sure I even know what really needs to be done, but I do know that the church is not reaching out to people in the area where it most should be, in the parishes. Priests can ill afford to insist that parishioners come to them. They must again offer to people what they have, assume a role of real leadership, show that Christ means love, that Christ is to be celebrated, that there is meaning to life and love after all—that there is more than frustration.

I do know of some parishes, some that are liberal, some experimental, some just showing plain common sense and a lot of sensitivity, that seem to have something going for

them, something vital, alive, real. A liturgy that really cele-
brates the Christ-event. The one instance I have particularly
in mind has a team of two priests whose primary work is to
prepare a living Sunday liturgy. (Imagine: two priests who
are not primarily teachers, counselors, committeemen, golf-
ers, or a combination of everything, but men of prayer,
leaders of prayer.) And though they are often criticized for
being theatrical, people flock to mass at their parish. They
must have something going. If a parish is to form any kind
of meaningful community, I feel, it has to have a vibrant
liturgy that invites people to keep coming back, to pray, to
worship together, to celebrate Christ with us.

I don't think we have attained that yet in our parish, but
I think we've begun something that ought to raise some
people's spirits. I'm looking for it to raise mine in any case.
I think it could snowball into a meaningful avenue of
prayer. At least that's what I hope, that's what I feel. Our
idea consists simply in offering to say mass in the homes of
the parishioners. We call it a home mass program. It has
nothing characteristic of the typical parish programs that
involve week after week of giving up time, effort or money
(the three stereotyped needs). And it's not such a revolutionary idea, really, because priests have been saying mass
in homes for quite some time. But people haven't been
asking them to, not generally anyway. I get enthused. I like
the idea. It could make the mass mean something to me
again personally.

It does have its drawbacks though. With all my enthusiasm, I'm only going to get one chance a year to have mass
celebrated in my home. We have three priests in our parish
and somewhere in the vicinity of fifteen to sixteen hundred

families. If the program really catches on (and with just a little encouragement it will), the three priests wouldn't be able to find days enough to effectuate the program they've begun. I'd love to see it come to that. It would support my feeling of the need for personal involvement in community prayer, in the mass. And it would recreate a spirit of vitality, interest and meaning.

But things don't happen fast in the church; they never have. Look how long it's taken for the church to realize its woes. The most recent statistics on church attendance available seem to show the dissatisfaction lay people have with church liturgies (but I get the impression the bishops don't believe in statistics). And with the total number of vocations tapering off too, it doesn't bode a good outlook: The church is looking more and more like a once supersuccessful company whose stocks are now plummeting rather than a divine institution that commands faith, love and obedience. And it's frustrating because I still believe a lot in the church and in what it stands for. It's not something I can easily turn my back on.

It's not my place, however, to say that the church, the parish, or the liturgy have out-and-out lost their meaning, their relevance. Too many changes after Vatican II were made for the sake of relevancy without enough preparation, and after the initial reactions the situation became worse than before. It's not the Latin Mass that I'm finding difficult to attend, it's the "renewed" English liturgy. But no matter what the changes had been in the liturgy over the past ten years, I think I would have lost my enthusiasm anyway without an accompanying change in attitudes toward worship. I am hoping that this home mass idea of

ours will do just that. It could even result in our priests being concerned primarily with worship and prayer again.
When they can effectively lead us in prayer we should regain
our enthusiasm about having them do so.

The impersonality of the way mass is often celebrated
bothers me a geat deal. Christianity can have such an impact on people: It preaches love of God and love of neighbor and that somehow the two are the same. It's a personal
religion. Christians are called on to show their love. God is
"Father." But our form of public worship isn't vibrant
enough. It doesn't reflect this impetus to love and it fails to
provide the motivation. For myself, it just doesn't relate
well enough to experience. It's as though I have to take time
out, put myself in a crowd (most of whom I don't know),
in order to worship. I don't get a feeling of real community
and I think some sense of that is important.

There are times when I prefer just being in a large congregation where I can keep my thoughts and feelings to myself, but not all the time. We have a large parish community
that is 99% "nominal" (that may be a bit harsh). Very few
people belong to the parish in the same way they do to their
family, their work group, the crowd they socialize with.
Within these circles they play an active part. The parish,
however, remains an all-encompassing kind of community
that includes many, many different communities—only
nominally, not actively. Like most parishioners I'm a parish-
ioner one hour of one day of each week. That doesn't give
me much to identify with.

This must have a lot to do with people not attending
mass as faithfully as in the past. Once there was more mystery, law, grace (?), even fear. Now the need is for mean-

ing and what is real. What I call a "nominal" parish needs to become something more than a spiritual service station. My feeling is that it has to become an active community; there has to be communication—outside of the "committee circuit," where for the most part the same small group of people show their interest in many different phases of parish life, from liturgy to education to pro-life.

If anyone is aware of the lack of communication in a parish it's the clergy. They have to eat, breathe, and sleep organized religion. Perhaps the hardest part of life in the "new church" for them is deciding what to do after all the pruning. So much has disappeared—all the devotions, novenas and benedictions and as yet there is nothing to replace them. People still expect the priests to provide them with their "religion." That is probably the toughest attitude to change; it just doesn't leave room for communication. And that's why liturgy committees that consist of both lay people and clergy are so important. That's where the new ideas, whether they originate there or not, are going to be evaluated and put into motion. We need good ideas. There have been good ideas that have led to effective changes in Sunday liturgies. Most progressive parishes all have good lay lectors, commentators, and singers. But mass is basically still a one-man-before-the-congregation ceremony and at the moment I don't see how it could be changed.

Each year new ideas come up that challenge the status quo or the attitudes of tradition. I think our idea-of-the-year, that of having masses regularly in the homes of the parishioners, if nothing else, will work on dispelling the attitude that it is the priest who supplies the religion. It will put a little initiative on both sides. I'm looking for it to add something to the liturgical life of the parish, for myself and for everyone. But big things happen little by little and it is yet to be seen if people are ready to bring the liturgy into their homes and leave the safety and passivity of the church. It is a challenge: getting to know new people, new personalities, even strangers, and showing them hospitality and friendship, and praying with them. But isn't that what Christianity is all about?

The home mass idea could answer a great need for me, and a great hope. I have attended many small-group masses in the past while I was still in school. Let me share one experience in particular: Together with about ten good friends I attended a prayer workshop. It was a unique experience for us all (and something I think everyone should experience), because as a group we shared prayer together and tried to learn something about prayer, about ourselves as pray-ers, how to pray, how to grow in prayer. I came away from that three-day experience with two things: I need to prepare myself to pray, and I can't isolate prayer from the rest of my life. It's something real; it's something I can grow in; it's something I need to share.

We compared our prayer forms to those of the Eastern religions. It sounds intellectual, but we found it very practical. While Catholics "go to mass" each Sunday and "pray" for an hour or so, believers in the Eastern religions spend about forty-five minutes putting themselves in the mood or spirit for every ten minutes they actually spend in prayer. We tried it. We chanted a simple rhythm together, we relaxed, we tried to put ourselves in the spirit of silent, relaxed meditation. Then we shared a few personal, intimate prayers. It was uplifting—and enjoyable. Prayer doesn't have to be something that can't be enjoyed. All too soon the weekend ended.

I've always remembered one conference from that workshop. Father Pete, the person in charge of coordinating the workshop, reflected on what's been happening to Americans and why it's so hard for young and old to worship together. I want to try to get it together again:

> Before World War II, especially the period after the Depression years, Catholics struggled to establish their parishes with good churches and schools and raise their families to enjoy all the freedoms they had dreamed of. The average American worked hard to secure his home, his family, his religion. Before anything else, his basic drive was for stability, establishing *security*.
>
> With the war, things changed; a new sentiment was being created; people were changing. The young rebelled against the old like never before. They had everything they could ever need, but in a sense they gave it up. What they wanted didn't come from a forty-hour week, owning one's own home, getting married, going to mass every Sunday, saying standard prayers and going through the same rituals over and over. Young people needed their own *identity* and they started looking for it elsewhere.

This was Father Pete's story, basically. (It's probably more as I remember it than as he actually told it to us then, but I've given the general feeling.) We came away from that conference thinking we had the bull by the horns. So that was it! The church was in trouble because people were in trouble. My father built my house and, in a sense, the church I was baptized in, and I was anxious to tear them both down. Didn't I want to be myself more than anything else? Didn't I know who I was? Wasn't I already out on my own? And wasn't I exhilarated at the discoveries I was making?

That was a stimulating stage of my life. I wanted to be a priest and I had already spent a number of years in the seminary. But it was an extremely confusing time, too. My companions and best friends were wrestling with similar questions. We were all learning to discover our feelings, recognize them, utilize them. It was a hard part of our training. I realized how much I had come to love one person, Jennifer, and it changed my life very suddenly. For others, the closeness of friendship and the solidification of purpose led them to be ordained. Most of us found something deep and meaningful and we all grew from the decisions we made and the responsibilities we accepted.

Our search for identity led us to be where we are now. I have often thought that Father Pete's theory of the change from the need for security to the need for identity is even more important than most of us realize. It certainly expresses a change in attitude that has been experienced, just the fact that people give more heed to their feelings than ever before. People are following their feelings, being themselves, and they rebel against being cogs in a machine. And as the statistics show the church is hardly exempt from it all. This change in attitude says a great deal about reduced church attendance, fewer vocations and the closing of schools and seminaries. I wonder, if a study were done on the religious phenomena of the 60s and 70s, how much the effects of this change in life-drives would explain the faltering of our establishments.

I grew up in a secure home, went to secure schools, and was able to secure a good career. I worried about "identity" long before I had to worry about "security." I had that luxury. There was always security and leadership in my school years, but I still look for certain kinds of leadership, and they are hard to find. I feel something's not quite right with society in general, with the church. Why do I scorn the institutions of church and government so much? Why am I distrustful in a crowded subway, on a dark street? Do I even believe anything can be done about it?

The lack of leadership in prayer, in church, is hard to do anything about, making it all the more frustrating. I could just drop out altogether but my Catholic background is so ingrained that I would probably feel guilty and I know it. My problem is that this is not what I want to do. I believe in the church, in what it could or should be, but how does one wait for it to start growing again.

I get enthused about mass in the homes. It's nothing revolutionary yet it's new and personal. And it's by no means a last resort. If it doesn't work out we'll look for a breath of fresh air in something else. But it does give our priests the chance to be leaders. They may never have the effect of Francis of Assisi or Martin Luther, but just maybe they'll be able to capture our spirits and help us restore some vigor to our worship. We might dispell some of the formality and impersonality and discover a little more what prayer and the mass are all about.

RUNNING . . . WITH
A LITTLE HELP

As director of the Detroit Archdio-
cese's Institute for Continuing Edu-
cation since 1966, JANE HUGHES
is probably the first woman in this
century to reach a top executive posi-
tion in the Catholic church. Much in
demand as a speaker, she has also
written and edited many educational
articles, television training programs,
and a public relations manual. Ms.
Hughes has served on many com-
mittees and commissions, including
the National Council of Catholic
Women, the Round Table of Chris-
tians and Jews, and the Detroit May-
or's Commission on Community
Relations. A native Detroiter, Ms.
Hughes and her husband have seven
children and eight step-children.

by Jane Hughes

I live yet not I, but Christ who dwells within me.
Gal. 2:20

BEING ON THE RUN, I FIND PEOPLE MUST SOMETIMES PUSH AT
me or shout to get my attention—but most of the time that
is not the case for God; as the expression goes, he is running
with me. There is no "on/off" switch in our communication
system . . . and furthermore, transmission is live.

The live-ness, liveliness and openness of the communication is perhaps the best description of my prayer life. It does
not mean that I exclude formal prayer, but rather the almost constant impromptu, alfresco kind of communication
I have has no form other than the fluid adaptability of the
moment. Formal prayer takes a willed action, the communication I am talking about is like breathing.

I've been living with the *we* mentality of Jesus and myself
for a long, long time. I can't really say when or how it happened. It's been in process since I was a young girl when a
natural spunkiness helped me to hold on to a meditative
kind of life I had developed on my own, despite the pressures to follow prescribed forms. I was also exceedingly for-

tunate to have had the strength to hold to the vision I had
of the Lord as Someone who loved me very much and who
was really concerned about me. Most of my friends thought
of God in terms of fear and the hell he was going to banish
them to if they were not good.

Over the years the relationship has continued to evolve
through tumult and passion, passivity and joy . . . much joy,
and its partner—suffering. Suffering is the mark of one who
loves Jesus. He disturbs me. He drives me, but he never
manipulates me. We have come a long way together.

My life is his life.

His truth is my truth.

At the center of me is Jesus.

The fact that I do not reflect that at all times, or even
part of the time, is my own human weakness. Even after all
this time, my way inward is slow and I keep finding greater
depths within myself. I am on a search of myself through
him to find the truth which is me. The more I know Christ,
the more I understand myself.

This knowledge did not come to me through study alone.
It came through a lifelong and honest searching for Christ,
an openness to his Spirit and by doing his will where and
when I meet him over and over again all my days.

I don't always get to Christ. If I place myself in the position of really being silent . . . he comes. It once was terribly
hard for me to reach that point of hearing only the silence
within me . . . of simply being. It still isn't easy but it is
taking place oftener and oftener. When I can turn into myself to rest silently, there comes to me a sense unlike anything I could create by myself. He is there and I know peace.

Today, theologians are presenting the hope of the resurrection as the vision of faith for our people. Certainly our hurting people must be given hope. I need it too but I need also to identify with the crucifixion. I need to consciously follow the example of Jesus in his suffering for others, realizing that this involves a process of consistently and constantly dying to myself.

I have learned that if I am to keep Jesus at the center of myself—if he is to live in me—I must crucify my ego. Otherwise there could be—and at times, there are—terrible battles!

The hardest thing in my life is to lose control over my life . . . to trust in him completely. My organizational ability is supposedly one of my greatest talents. It is also one of my greatest stumbling blocks. It is prefectly natural to attempt to organize my life. Yet, his wishes for me *constantly* mess up my plans. The death of my ego must come in order for me to be reborn. I know this, but I don't always accept it and even when I do accept it, it is never with enthusiasm.

Your ways, O Lord, make known to me; teach me your paths. Ps. 25:4

The evolving relationship with Jesus has been an intensely personal journey. Directional signs were so often my own reactions, failings, strengths, mistakes, hurts, dreams and joys. Yet, all along I have been very conscious of the danger of making him into my image: Jane's personal God . . . with attributes she thinks a God should have and acting the way she thinks a God should act. Consequently, all my life I have gone to spiritual writers and to the scriptures. The latter I now go to daily at some time or other. Then too, and even more clearly, I have found his image in others. There is nothing unusual in finding the first reflection of him in your parents. In my parents I not only saw him in them, I saw them habitually turning to him in prayer and service. Both were a way of life with them, not something which was nice to do when you had the time and the inclination to do so.

Growing up in an extended family whose lives were devoted to rebuilding the world through the church, I knew and developed friendships with intensely committed persons . . . those in church leadership, those who began movements and those who were bent on tearing up the old institutions. I met Christ in those who were being helped— the poor, the oppressed and the misunderstood. Certainly these people had an influence on my spiritual life. Many still do, for I continue to work with those whose lives are a commitment to the cause of Christ. They are devoted people of God . . . using themselves up for him.

I could not have managed my own life of commitment in this way—and perhaps not at all—if I had not been blessed with two exceptional men as husbands. In each case, it was their goodness which attracted me and which supported me in the life I was called to lead. Our relationship was and is an extension of each of our relationships with Christ.

My spiritual reading was a long series of gropings . . . of using some ideas as bases for my own building and finding a lot that I couldn't accept as my own. Always present—and I don't know where it came from—was a real horror of any taint of what I thought to be phoniness or unnaturalness in spirituality. So I was a wary reader, listener and doer.

However,I traveled the gamut of spiritual reading that I suppose is traveled by most Catholic youth who are seeking God either by personal desire or persuasion: the racks of pious pamphlets to St. Ignatius in the younger days, through *Integrity* and *The Catholic Worker* to the vast amounts of writings produced today. In the past, three writers came into my life at crucial points of need for spiritual inspiration: Cardinal Emmanuel Suhard, Dom Van Zeller and Thomas Merton. I read everything I could find of the first two, most of Merton. They were practical in their approaches to holiness and never lowered their objectives. As the Cardinal wrote in his spiritual diary: *"To be a saint, therefore, must be our unique objective."*

Writings by and about the saints helped me to see my life in the perspective of holiness as a friend of Christ. I went to them at different times and for different lifestyles.

A clearer mirror for me now of man's eternal struggle for God is in the theater and the film. Naturally I don't mean the trite . . . but those superbly done vehicles which lash you about in your responses to their messages. They make me ache with and for the suffering Christ and I have no trouble hearing the clarity of the call for my commitment. *Hey look at me, hey look at me!*—come the unvoiced cries of the crucified Christ in the bumbling, driven, scared Willie Lomans and from the heroic pretenses and alienation of the Amanda Wingfields . . . and I look around and find them, and listen to them. The terrible thing in our society is that they are everywhere and as in one of Michel Quoist's prayers, they will absorb your life if you let them. These people are one of the great dilemmas of my life. As they come, do I say, *Yes Lord,* or *I've got this other thing I must do for someone else needing me.* The problem is not selfishness as opposed to charity. No, it has come to a point where I must make a decision as to which of the two I must serve.

> *For God is at work in you, both to will and to work for*
> *His good pleasure.*
> Phil. 2:3

I have no problem with the fact that God is working through me. It is a condition I have accepted and it is the only reason that could have moved me to reveal myself in this essay, which I have found very difficult to put into words. In the past, in other such instances, he has allowed me invisibility, which is a lot more comfortable.

Twenty years ago I wrote a long series of spiritual meditations for a Catholic journal. They were published anonymously because it was thought that even though they were intended for the laity, they would lose authenticity if it were known that they were a reflection of a *laywoman's* spiritual yearnings and gropings. They were received well by the many who wrote letters about them, all addressed: *Dear Father.*

I have learned that being an instrument of the Lord— *and* being a woman—has called forth practically all the virtues. This strange subjugation of womanhood by the church has not existed in my relationship with Jesus. I have to apologize to him about a lot, but never for being a woman. Actually the security I have known with him has allowed me to walk with grace through the years of situations where the hurts could have broken me. Coming from that unquestioned acceptance gave me the impetus to move ahead with a great deal less emotionalism and hostility than are being shown in our time. This doesn't mean that I stepped back at any time but that I could be quieter about it. From my secret place within me I could watch with amusement, knowing that sooner or later, things would change . . . and they have.

Then too, the example of unwavering womanly strength and courage of Mary, my intimate friend and confidante, has been my lighthouse in all kinds of seas. Her "yeses" in the face of the unknown move me off the edge of timidity and self-pity which I may approach as a woman in a man's world.

> *Out of the depths I cry to you, O Lord; Lord, hear my voice!*
>
> Ps. 130:1

Prayer rises from the depths . . . at least those prayers do which have the greatest meaning for me. (Others are more like companionable conversing which, in their own way, say *I love you.*) Prayer comes from the fullness of joy in him or others . . . from the deepness of pain . . . the agony over hurting him . . . from the bubbling up feeling of thanksgiving, from a dredging down to pull out the reasons for asking for his help.

My prayer changes all the time . . . but the process is the same. It is a meeting, a coming together. It is not so much me praying *to* Christ as Christ's praying within me. He takes my joys, agonies, mistakes, problems and hopes and transforms them by his prayer. I have come to see that he is about his work of bringing my personal life to his Father in his mission of redeeming the world. That he should have so much concern for me is utterly beyond comprehension. Sometimes I feel as though I were exploding with joy inside that he has allowed me to know what little I do about him.

I have tried some methods of physically preparing myself to pray and for entering into prayer, but have not yet found one which makes me feel comfortable. It could be that I did not give them enough of a chance, but I can't circumvent my acute consciousness of positioning myself. My body becomes bigger than my prayer, so I do not use any methods as such.

This impediment could be a residue left from the Lenten schooldays of saying the stations. There was so much concentration placed on genuflecting and standing that the drama of the fourteen illustrations was lost to me at that time. On my own I would go back into church, in the dark back pews under the shadow of the rose window, and talk out his passion and death with him. That is still the way I say the stations but not always in church.

There is no question now that I *must* draw back from the presence of others, to collect myself, to pull strength from knowing I am . . . and to increase my sense of awe of his presence within me. Christ being so constantly my dearest companion I fear I do not show sufficient appreciation or, even worse, forget who he is. I would hate to hear him say, ". . . you have less love now than you used to."

There is the need to draw away from others so that my repentance is honest and full. It is easier to make excuses when there are distractions.

This brings me to the best time for prayer for me: that most private moment of the day when I first awaken . . .

before my eyes let in the light . . . right after I leave the dream world to enter reality. Then we truly talk.

I love you Lord; thank you for keeping me alive . . .
Another day . . . what are we going to do with it?

It is in those private moments—which sometimes last as long as a half hour—that I examine my conscience. (At night I find I do a slipshod job of examination. My usual weariness, pushed to its utmost by the drive of my frustrations to do one more thing in that day, prevents any objective review.) Did I say "yes" to those in need . . . when they needed it? Was he hurt because of what I said or did? How did I handle that ever-present tension of the inward-outward conflict of what I felt I should do and what I did do?

These questions are just too much at night. In the morning I can cope. We go over the needs of those closest to me: the child who needs more loving . . . the one who has been churning up turmoil among the others . . . why? . . . the relative who needs to be needed . . . etc., etc., etc.

It is at this time that I treasure his love the most and I see that it makes all other loves possible. All these loves are my problem as well as my treasure. How can I serve them all? Then there is a sifting out of what really can be done. And I have to laugh to myself because there will be so many more demands upon me during the many hours to come.

Throughout the day I try to re-create this privacy. I drive to and from work alone. The cocoon of the car is good but the same concentration is impossible. Yet even with its lack, it is a good place to pray. Flying alone brings me most vividly into his presence . . . so does the anonymity of the medical reception rooms where everyone sits patiently, an island to himself.

I never sit down at the typewriter without asking for inspiration from the Holy Spirit. There are times when even he can't help me, especially during those dry periods which are the bane of creative effort. I should mention that I have always been conscious of the Holy Spirit working in me when I was involved in creative work . . . and in making decisions about that work. It was with a sense of adventure that I would turn to him for help. I have learned that with his support I can be more daring than I would possibly be on my own.

I will not leave you desolate; I will come back to you.
John 14:18

At the time of my first husband's death, I held onto those words. He left one morning and didn't come home again. He was killed instantly in an automobile accident. We never saw him again. The strength with which I met the next two months was partly due to the solid and natural relationship I had with Christ—and partly the shock was still dulling my reactions.

As time went on and the shock wore off and the dailyness of living without my husband made me pull back from life, I found also that I was pulling back from Christ. The easiness of relationships I had enjoyed all my life was not so much strained as it just wasn't there. The dark night of the soul had set in. This was a condition I did not choose and was unable to change. It was the greatest loneliness. I was alone inside and out. While Christ did not come to me in the usual way, he did keep his promise not to leave me. He sent two to strengthen me, and they brought me through.

> *All of us, gazing on the Lord's glory with unveiled faces, are being transformed from glory to glory into his very image by the Lord who is the Spirit.*   Cor. 3:18

After my dear father's death, my reactions were so different. The loss was there, my daily habits changed but I had been involved in the process of seeing him transformed. As I sat with him through the weeks of his leaving, death became not so strange or ominous.

He was able to bring a certain amount of self-direction and a great deal of dignity to the process of dying. Death did not come to him, he moved to it. He knew he was dying. He accepted it. My brother's and my last words to him were, "*We love you Papa.*" His last lip-formed message (as his voice box was almost gone with the cancer which had eaten all but his spirit) was, *I love you too.* He was smiling, at peace.

It was a profound experience that I am grateful to have had, and all through it I walked deeper and deeper inside myself and Christ was with me all the way.

> *Your light must shine before men so that they may see goodness in your acts and give praise to your heavenly father.*   Mt. 5:16

As in my parent's life, mine has been one of prayer and service. They belong together. My response to God and my social responsibility are one. It's like a loop. I journey in-

wards in prayer and come back out again to express my love
of Christ in caring for my brothers and sisters in him. With
the intensive activity of my life there are times when I feel
like a juggler with too many plates in the air but somehow
able to maintain a certain balance. That balance is possible
because of my prayer life.

In my work with groups devoted to action, I am finding a
swing back to the recognition of the need for prayer. For a
while every energy was poured forth for the cause into action. Now many are finding that the life of action and its
effectiveness is wearing thin because the work did not stem
from the root of a Christ-relationship.

> *Where two or three are gathered in my name, there I*
> *am in their midst.*   Mt. 18:20

While this essay speaks primarily about private prayer,
my life needs and, yes, yearns for prayer together with
others.

The definite and necessary partnership between prayer
and social responsibility is no less needed between private
prayer and that which brings many persons together, showing their love for God at the same time. For me, personal
prayer alone would eventually lose the sense of awe and
celebration and mystery. This would hurt me and certainly
hurt my relationship with Jesus. I need those qualities in my
life. In fact, I believe we need more of them in our daily
lives which are swiftly becoming more drab and flat.

I also hunger for the sense of community gained by praying with others. When my family come to the meal table
to share in prayer, in addition to the affectionate convivi-

ality and eating, I relish the sharing of the prayer which puts the rest into context. When I participate in the liturgy I am strongly aware of all who surround me and form the worshiping community. I am proud to be there. I am uplifted and comforted by it. I feel a need not only to receive this sense of support, but to give it.

While I have spoken little of the extremely complex life I lead, the reader will gain that insight from the brief biography at the beginning of my essay. In light of this insight I hope that what I have said makes clear that I feel that a deep relationship with Jesus does not mean an escape into a kind of heaven on earth or a world confined to good persons. While I have not alluded to it, I cannot make trivial the evil which is evident in our world: violence, dishonesty, misuses of persons and the hurts which come from them. I feel deeply my responsibility to bring God's reconciling love to that world.

The goal of my prayers then is not to receive something or even to find peace and happiness but to become more like Christ and to do his will.

HANGING IN . . . WITH PASCAL AND THE NEW YORK TIMES

As *managing editor of* Commonweal, *JOHN DEEDY is a perceptive commentator on American religious and secular life. With Martin Marty and David Silverman he wrote* The Religious Press in America. *He edited* Eyes on the Modern World *and is the author of* What A Modern Catholic Believes About Conscience, Freedom and Authority *and the soon-to-be-published* What A Modern Catholic Believes About The Commandments. *A frequent contributor to the* New York Times *and* The Critic, *Mr. Deedy and his family live in Larchmont, New York.*

by John Deedy

IT'S ANTI-INTELLECTUAL, I CONCEDE. IT SMACKS OF SPIRITUAL pragmatism and pragmatic skepticism—however you wish to twist the idea. Nevertheless, these days there's something subtly enticing about Pascal's wager. Pascal's wager doesn't suit traditionalists . . . never did. And it doesn't suit iconoclastic intellectuals, as Michael Harrington makes unmistakably clear in his autobiographical book *Fragments of the Century*. Yet Pascal's wager is assuredly providing many believers with a handle for hanging in during these unsettling times for religion. As much as I try to resist the notion of Pascal's wager, I don't figure I'm about to rub it out of my psyche.

Like Mike Harrington, I came in contact with Pascal's wager when I was a student at Holy Cross College in Worcester, Mass., back in the 1940s. Pascal's wager wasn't presented to me and my classmates for laying away in our intellectual or our spiritual treasury. It was floated over our heads like a fat blimp, and then neatly shot down, probably by syllogism; I don't recall exactly. But this I do remember: In the intellectual and spiritual posturing of our youth some of us packed Pascal's wager into a grab bag of information, thereafter to be pulled out in barrooms and during beach-blanket conversations where there were folks to be impressed. It proved a wonderfully effective item, provided the objects of our erudition were as uninformed as we considered ourselves informed, which was not always the case. With a little luck, though, we emerged both knowing and skeptical—to us a delightful, if somewhat contradictory, combination of qualities.

The world of Catholicism was in its orderly orbit in the 1940s, and faith was something most of us came by implicitly. There needed to be no wagering about whether there was or was not a God. In such a milieu, a dash of skepticism had an almost exhilarating effect. Or so we persuaded ourselves. Anyway, when the talk got around to God and religion, as it inevitably did, Pascal's wager was wheeled in (a) as a kind of cosmic explanation for our very uncosmic religious status, and (b) as indication of our religious daring and spiritual independence. After all, weren't we indirectly questioning accepted teaching and directly identifying with a theological maverick—a big, bad man? Not that Pascal was all that bad. He was a Jansenist and a Jesuit-baiter, but he died in what our old *Catholic Encyclopedia* told us was an "ecstasy of joy" after having received "the Holy Viaticum"—which, of course, was an ending we secretly applauded. Death-bed reconciliations with God and death-bed reaffirmations of faith provided consolations and quickened Catholic convictions far and wide in those days. They were proofs all their own of the authenticity of the Roman Catholic religion.

In any case, we played our games with Pascal's wager. If the terms of that wager have slipped anyone's mind, this (with the help of the aforementioned encyclopedia) is the way Pascal's wager goes:

> God exists or he does not exist, and one must of necessity lay odds for or against this existence.

> If one wagers *for* — and God exists—infinite gain; and God does not exist—no loss.

> If one wagers *against* — and God exists—infinite loss; and God does not exist—neither loss nor gain.

> In the second of the wager's alternatives, one is exposed to the loss of everything. Therefore one does not take it. Wisdom instead dictates the first wager, since it assures winning all or, at worse, losing nothing.

Now, as I've indicated, when we were propounding Pascal's wager in the 1940s, we possessed certitude of knowledge with respect to faith and religion. We had in our repertoire all the hard proofs for the existence of God—the deductive and inductive proofs, the *a priori* and *a posteriori* arguments. The proofs were exact—and, of course, impressive—but not exciting. Alongside them, Pascal's wager was dashing. We stored it in, as one might supplement a healthy diet with a vitamin pill that wasn't at all needed. In storing it, some of us must also have assimilated it, at least in part. I'm prepared to be told that I belong in that category.

When I was approached about contributing a chapter to

this book on the maintenance of one's spiritual life, one of
the first thoughts to come to mind was of Pascal—probably
because before one presumed to speak of the spiritual life,
one had first to confirm belief itself, a detail I don't believe
I troubled about for years.

The question of belief proved no problem. I easily con-
firmed to myself that I do believe. But, I asked, do I believe
with Pascal as a crutch? There I was given pause . . . But
then, I asked, would that be so terribly cynical? Is Pascal's
wager so foolish, so unreasonable when one lives at a moment of church history in which the givens of the faith are
being stripped away right and left? Maybe not.

Nowadays I have the feeling that, wittingly or not, the
intellectual plaything of my early-20s is now an I-beam of
my religious faith (I-beam, as distinct from cornerstone).
For one thing, it's so much easier to take Pascal's wager that
God exists than to rout the uncertainties of an age in which
the book of one's religion has been rewritten by going back
and reviewing the old proofs. It's simpler to let be what is,
and resolve the uncertainties by wagering along with Pascal
(even if it's only a side-bet).

Admittedly, there's nothing theologically or scientifically
intellectual in such an attitude. Indeed, if one is a reflex
Catholic, it could return the believer, in effect, to the me-
chanical mode of yesterday: To the fulfilling of the rules
and the prerequisites—protecting the bet, in other words, in
order to insure the payoff. Then, isn't one right back where
one started in the 1940s? . . . Not necessarily. There's still a
lot of room for individuality. Pascal's own life is evidence of
this, in the event you care to check it out, and, naturally,
make the allowance that he won his wager. Pascal was any-

thing but a programmed believer. Nevertheless, I concede that a certain minimum observance of rules and regulations is imposed on one by taking Pascal's route.

But back to belief . . . I believe in addition, I discovered, for the untranscendental reason that I feel it important to belong to a particular tradition and culture—and Catholic tradition (for all its faults) and Catholic culture (for all its easy libeling) are mine by birth and, as far as I can see, as worthwhile as any others on which I have a choice. Perhaps more worthwhile.

Besides, I'm a creature of Western civilization, and Western civilization, Catholic tradition and Catholic culture are in too many ways inseparable—for me, as for Belloc. Thus to reject Catholic tradition and culture would be for me to separate myself not only from faith, but also from what the poet Ned O'Gorman calls the great mythology of signs, rituals, poetry, drama, art, music and all the other facets of that civilization, tradition and culture. I wouldn't want to do that. I may not hear a Mozart Mass any more in the churches I visit, or a Gregorian chant. But when I catch either, whether on the radio station of the *New York Times* or in some exalted music hall, I want to be able to identify spiritually as well as appreciate aesthetically. I could do that in a vacuum of belief, I suppose. Many people do. But I'll grant them their experience, and make my choice.

All this having been said—and getting down now to the concretes of spiritual life—a confession is in order: Like all Catholics (am I using others to excuse myself?), I pray less. There's no longer any rushing to confession before an airplane trip, no longer a whipping out of the rosary at the start of a long automobile journey, no whispered appeal to the "appropriate" saint at minor moments of anxiety.

Not only do I pray less, but I sometimes wonder whether my regular attendance at Sunday mass is due to pure devotion, or is it to be traced to a desire to set an example for the children, or to unconscious habit, or to some other imperfect impulse? I suppose elements of these factors and more come into play, singly and collectively. Self-analysis tends to impart my motivations to the less noble possibilities. On the other hand, I know that at times of great stress —the death of a friend, for instance, or the illness of a relative—the immediate instinct is to think of God and the eternal, to pray, and to head in the direction of a church. In a real way, this instinct is inner confirmation that I do genuinely believe—and believe in Catholicism, since it is to a Catholic church that I'll make my way in times of personal crisis. I don't think it ever occurs to me to pop into a Protestant church in anxious moments—which is probably an unecumenical confession to make. (I do frequently visit Protestant churches, and while there I do pray. But it is usually the special occasion of a wedding or a funeral, or the desire to sightsee, that brings me there in the first place.)

At the same time, it is confirmation (and consolation) to me of the faith of my children, when at critical moments in their own young lives they ask their mother to say a particular prayer or novena of prayers for their intentions (the children, like most young folks these days, being too busy to pray themselves, and, I suppose, somehow not trusting the power of their father's prayers in quite the same way as they do their mother's—not an uncommon phenomenon).

What I'm owning up to, I guess, is the admission that there likely is a degree of bravado in my religious attitudes, and, if I am typical at all, in that of my allegedly skeptical friends as well. (I have one friend, by way of example, who is offhand about his religious practices, scornful of religious authority, and resentful about much of the religious fare on which he was brought up, such as holy candles. Yet, a few months back, when he learned that an intimate of his had been hit by a heart attack, he rushed from his office to a church, where he lighted a bank of holy candles. Well, one at least. The point is that he did in a moment of concern what he had been scoffing at for years. Was he acting out of superstition, or genuine belief, or Pascalian impulse? He probably couldn't answer himself.)

One problem of mine is that when I get into church, whether for a Sunday liturgy or on a chance visit, I find myself after some minutes somewhat unprayerful and eventually devoid of most spiritual impulses. My mind wanders. I fail to catch the words that come to me from the pulpit. I lose track of the reason that brought me to church in the first place. I find myself at the end of a prayer with no recollection of passing through its middle part. Naturally, I don't blame myself for this slipshod devotion. I blame the performance of the priest, the shallowness of the service, noise or other factors, although deep down there is a consciousness that the blame must also be mine. Then, too, there's that easy target, the new liturgy. I'm afraid it hasn't added much to my spiritual life. (I miss for one thing, I find, that touch of theater of which I was so contemptuous in the past, but which I now realize had the effect at least of attracting and occupying my attention.) The sum of all this is a certain personal disenchantment. I wonder whether I have lapsed into a state of faith without real devotion—

not a fatal condition spiritually, but not an exactly healthy one either.

On the other hand, the new liturgy isn't always for me a lost hour. A reverent and relevant mass can give me considerable spiritual uplift—as, for instance, when the celebrant relates the reading of the mass to some public or personal concern, or when he personalizes the ceremony at moments like the reception of Communion ("Body of Christ, John"), or when some warm person puts real Christian feeling into the exchange of greetings during the Communion rite. This is relatively rare, though. Most of the time I leave mass without conscious uplift, and, furthermore, without the cultural gratification that the Latin frequently supplied in the old days. I allow instantly that the mass is not intended to be a cultural experience, or an intellectual one either—at least not in the pure sense. But if the mass had such dimensions, as it surely did with the Latin, what complaint can there be? I say all this without arguing at the same time for any wholesale return to the Latin. I favor the vernacular, but a vernacular that does not insult what intelligence I possess and chill me spiritually in the process.

By way of aside (and to say what so many others have already said), I am convinced that one of the greatest tragedies of reform and renewal is that there was not a Ronald Knox or a stylist of similar talent on hand to manage the translation of the English vernacular. The deeper we get into the vernacular period, the more jejune seem the readings. And then the syntax! Listen carefully next time at mass to the eucharistic doxology: "Through him, with him, in him, in the unity of the Holy Spirit, all honor and glory is yours, almighty father. . . ." There's a verb usage that is close to being a matter for the confessional.

What I'm saying, I guess, is what Rosemary Radford Ruether said some time ago in the British journal, *The Month:* The vernacularization of the liturgy now appears in retrospect to have been an ambiguous accomplishment. We got a mass that we could at last understand *in toto*, but one that added little or nothing to our spiritual lives. Certainly this is true so far as my spiritual life is concerned. And I fear that I will continue to be put off until someone who can handle the English language—really handle it— takes up pen and redoes the translation. Looking back now, the mistake seems to have been made in making vernacularization a matter solely for the ecclesiastical professionals; a writer or two—believer or nonbeliever—should have been included in the project. They might have saved us from a botched job.

Of course, I've got to admit that I don't give my spiritual life the supplementary assists that I once did. The family Bible is dusty. Thomas à Kempis isn't on the bedside table anymore. I haven't made a retreat since I got caught in one during the Cuban missile crisis. My spiritual reading has been replaced almost completely by "issue" books—books by Hans Küng, Eugene Kennedy, Garry Wills and other writers addressing themselves to topical questions and current church developments. Books on the spiritual life are at something of a nadir these days, they say. But this does not account for the shifts in my reading emphases—not completely anyway. Mine is the lot of the communicator. I read issue books because of the necessity to "keep up." If there are only so many hours in a day, what other choice do I have? (I'm rationalizing out loud now.)

Having said all this, from where do I get the nourishment without which belief and one's spiritual life would wither?

Mostly, I'd say, from the example of certain individuals. . . .
From the Dorothy Days working among the down-and-outs.
From the Dan Berrigans asserting the rights of conscience
against the laws of the state. From the James Groppis and
the Cesar Chavezes championing the causes of the poor and
the put-upon. From the Robert Drinans holding public
office and worrying less about their futures than about a set
of principles. From intellectuals—the Christopher Dawsons
and the Jacques Maritains (Maritain's last years notwithstanding)—whose strength of mind adds to a strengthening
of faith.

It is from people such as these, people working out of an
explicit Christological reference, that I draw the principal
inspirations of my spiritual life in this, my middle age. I
note that the secular humanist can do (and sometimes does
better) many or all the things that the people of my inspiration are doing. But for me a dimension is lacking in the
secular humanist—specifically that dimension of supernatural inspiration which takes a human act and, through a
Gospel context, raises it to another level. Presence with a
difference, as current spirituality might describe it.

Thus it is that I can derive as much inspiration from a
New York Times news story involving someone who is present to his or her contemporaries in a Christological context
as I can from some liturgies, and more than I might glean
from almost any traditional book of spiritual reading.
Maybe all this is shallow and silly, but there it is.

What this means is that my spiritual life is based today,
not on the props of the past, so much as it is on that thing
called presence—presence, which observed in others both
inspires and motivates. How do you recognize presence? Let

Ecuador's Bishop Proano tell us: "Presence . . . means knowledge of reality. Not a purely intellectual knowledge, but a knowledge based on direct contact with life's realities, on involvement with the problems of the man in the street, on sharing the worries and hopes of the people. That sort of knowledge means taking part in the construction of the material world, of the world of men. Direct contact, activity, involvement, successes and failures—these are indispensable ingredients in a genuine knowledge. Presence also means constant confrontation with the unexpected. It is just the opposite of escapism, withdrawal, tranquillity. Presence means signing up for desperate struggles, dangerous gambles, unpleasant ventures. Presence means standing shoulder to shoulder with people who are suffering."

The atheist or agnostic who is "present" to the world also inspires and motivates, and I do not wish to deny that for a second. Still, there remains for me a difference, as indefinable as it may be to everyone's satisfaction, between the presence of the secular humanist and the presence of the person whose witness is leavened by some quality of the supernatural.

There should be nothing wondrous about this kind of evaluating, nothing strange about the internal spiritual application—not insofar as a Catholic like myself is concerned. The urgency of an expanded and sharpened Christological presence in the world is why so many placed such large hopes in Vatican Council II and its schema on the Church in the Modern World. That schema emerged from the Council as a pastoral constitution dealing with the very sorts of activities that the committed are today caught up in. If it is incongruous, therefore, to speak of the witness of

the intellectual, the social activist and others as being in-
spirational and as contributing to one's spiritual life, then
we may as well rub the Constitution on the Church in the
Modern World off the history books of religion and out
of the Catholic experience.

LIVING WITH
THE TENSIONS

ROBERT NOWELL is an English journalist who was assistant editor of the Tablet *(London) from 1962 to 1967 and editor of the now-defunct* Herder Correspondence *from 1968 until 1970. He has contributed to numerous publications and is a regular correspondent for the* Catholic Review *(Baltimore). He is the author of* The Ministry of Service: Deacons in the Contemporary Church, What A Modern Catholic Believes About Death *and the forthcoming* What A Modern Catholic Believes About Mysticism. *He and his family live outside London.*

by Robert Nowell

TRADITIONAL CATHOLIC SPIRITUALITY WAS NEVER BRED INTO me, so that shaking myself lose from it must have been easier for me than for many. Of course, when I became a Catholic at the age of twenty I tried to fit myself into the new mold. I acquired a rosary, disciplined myself to going to confession fairly regularly, learned what the stations of the cross were and sometimes went to benediction. But the new mold never really fit, and it was a relief when I came to realize that being a Catholic didn't mean having to conform to one particular pattern. If I found saying the rosary unhelpful, an attempt to numb the mind by vain repetitions such as the heathen use, then this didn't mean I was a bad Catholic or no Catholic at all. It simply meant I was a different kind of Catholic.

Yet I find myself up against the same problem as that faced by those for whom the decay of traditional spirituality has been a traumatic experience. There's a danger of failing to replace what was old and unsatisfactory with something new and better, a danger intensified by the fact that for almost all of us it has come to be very much a do-it-yourself operation—and in my particular case a danger further intensified by a strong streak of laziness. But even when one is faced with the bleak prospect of emptiness—of leaving a house swept and garnished for seven other spirits more wicked than the first—even then the old magic will no longer work.

For the difficulties go to the heart of what is meant by that traditional term "the spiritual life." Prayer itself has become problematical. We thought of prayer in terms of talking to someone up there—our own private hot-line to the Holy Spirit. And that kind of imagery just won't work anymore. I find I am more and more uncertain about who or what God is, while at the same time I am more and more certain that he exists—that there is a personal, fiercely loving power underpinning and giving meaning to the confused jumble of events we experience as the world. In the same way I believe that this power revealed itself in human terms in the man Jesus, and that in the resurrection of Jesus we are given the ultimate assurance that this human life of ours does have meaning, however futile and trivial it may seem, and that the final enemy of death has been overcome. More: The Spirit is at work in human history, and can be discerned wherever suspicion gives way to reconciliation, hatred to love, and hope is able to build again.

All this reduces much of what I used to think of as prayer to the level of idle chatter. Instead, prayer is surely far more a question of listening. After all, the whole purpose of the exercise is twofold. One is to enable me to cope with myself, to prevent the selfish I from getting in the way of the real I, so that when the moment comes that I am called on to respond to the Christ that is in other people I am able to do so instead of twisting their needs to my ends and ex-

ploiting them. The other is to learn to hear the voice of the
Lord in the human situation; for that, surely, is the way the
Lord speaks to his people.

Now, that can't be described as what I am aiming at. I've
already mentioned a strong streak of laziness in my make-up.
It would be fairer to say it's what from time to time I'm
aware I should be aiming at. And again, if I go on to talk
about the means that might help me to get there, it's more
a question of what I could do if I had the energy and the
single-mindedness to get my priorities right: "Seek ye first
the kingdom of God, and his righteousness."

Besides laziness, there's another obstacle in my personal
make-up. For a long time I've been aware that too much
concentration on the spiritual life defeats its own object as
far as I'm concerned. I've only ever made one retreat, and
that lasted only four days. And it wasn't just laziness that
made me realize in my early days as a Catholic that it was
no use my trying to go to daily mass as a Lenten exercise—
or, come to that, at any other time of the year. The effect
of overindulgence in the spiritual is to make me start react-
ing violently against it. This may simply prove that basically
I'm irreligious and irreverent, but I don't think that's the
point. What I think is involved here is a largely unconscious
protest against the gap that can all too easily open up between the other-world of the spiritual life and the here-and-
now world that, to my mind at least, Christianity must be
about if it is to mean anything. For me, the spiritual life
is not a way of cutting oneself off from the world, but a way
of becoming more effectively involved in it.

This temperamental obstacle ties in with a peculiarity of
the kind of life I live; and that is that for most of the past

fifteen years my work has been concerned with religion. As
a Catholic journalist I was on the staff of the *Catholic
Herald,* then assistant editor of *The Tablet,* then editor of
Herder Correspondence; and now as a freelance writer I
find that my major saleable skill is precisely my knowledge
of the religious scene. Often my work has built into it what
can almost be described as a devotional element. That is,
it can demand of me worrying out what the Gospel demands of us in a certain aspect of our lives and trying to
explain this clearly to myself and to others. Writing this
contribution to this book is one example: It is forcing me
to think deeply about an aspect of my life which, as I have
already made clear, I would be only too happy to ignore.
Another was having to write about death for the *What A
Modern Catholic Believes* . . . series: Writing that book
was a salutary experience, because I had to grapple with an
issue which is central to the Christian faith but which I had
always shied away from thinking about.

Of course, the devotion is built into the work, and in that
way it's easy for me. It's not a question of distracting myself
with self-consciously pious thoughts while my hands cope
with a boring job, or trying to keep my balance while
attempting to persuade myself and my colleagues that it's
vitally important for several thousand more housewives to
buy a particular brand of margarine or washing-powder. In
that way I've been able to opt out of the dilemma facing so
many people: That their work, whether on the assembly
line or in something like an advertising agency, has so little
apparent relevance to the basic business of being human.

But the kind of work I am engaged in has its disadvan-
tages too. One is that it's irregular. It varies from day to

day and from week to week, from reporting, which can often consist of long periods of boredom interspersed with short bursts of intense activity, to the kind of writing I'm involved in now, which demands sustained and concentrated reflection. The other is that it's largely concerned with religion, which means that to develop an intense spiritual life on traditional lines would lead me straight into the risk of the strong reaction I've just mentioned to overindulgence in the spiritual. As a good part of my waking preoccupations are with the Gospel and the church, to go on to devote time to private spirituality wouldn't involve the relief and the change that it must for many people.

This was brought home to me when, between working on the *Catholic Herald* and *The Tablet*, I spent an enjoyable fifteen months or so as a subeditor with *TV Times*, the program journal for British commercial television. My job was to make up the program pages for one of the regional editions and see that all the details were correct. It was very much a routine nine-to-five (or rather ten-to-six) job with nothing in it to carry home with one: It was work that didn't spill over into the rest of my life but left me free to develop other interests outside. During this period I not only learned that I wasn't meant to be a novelist by trying to write a novel, but I also got into the habit of reading the hours of the Office each day, from Lauds through to Compline. I had the leisure, too, to start exploring the Fathers of the Church: Ignatius, Polycarp, some Ambrose and Jerome. I even started plowing through Augustine's *Enarrationes in Psalmos*. But starting work on *The Tablet* soon put a stop to all that: I never found out what Augustine had to say about all the psalms beyond number 31 or

32. It was just more than I could fit in with a job which demanded my whole attention, which spilled over into the rest of my life, and which was concerned with religion.

So what am I left with? Basically, the liturgy. For me, common worship is fundamentally what Christian spirituality is all about. Christianity is about other people, about our relations with each other, and there seems to be something wrong if it leads to overmuch concentration on oneself and one's own individual problems. True, these have to be faced up to and dealt with, but in the context of trying to live out and give expression to the fundamental Christian ideal of love of neighbor, of learning how to respond simply and genuinely to other people's needs, of helping everyone to become the kind of person he or she is meant to be. There's nothing very private about trying to be a Christian.

This was brought home to me by another episode. About five years ago, I found myself taking part in a five-day study conference on authority in the church, at a time when I was feeling rather fed up with that institution and with things in general. I thought I was going as a dispassionate observer, simply to report on an event from outside. To my surprise I found myself becoming completely involved. And it was a question of total immersion—listening to the various papers presented, taking part in the discussions, both formal and informal, making new friends, sharing each day in the Eucharist. In fact, it was the first time that I felt— as opposed to merely paying lip-service to an intellectual proposition—that it would be utterly wrong not to share in the Eucharist. What had happened was that for the first time I had been able to experience the church as community. And I was able to bring this experience away with

me, to come back with a revitalized faith in the church. I
learned that it was no use just sitting back and complaining
that the church didn't measure up to my expectations without doing anything about it. Being a Christian—like being
married—was something one had to work at with the other
people involved.

So the core of my spiritual life is Sunday worship—join-
ing in the prayers and hymns, listening to the readings from
the Bible. It's much easier now, of course, than it was when
I first became a Catholic twenty-odd years ago. The public
dimension is no longer hidden. But even in the old days I
took a certain participation for granted. My first real contact with the church was the Oxford university chaplaincy,
where dialogue Mass was the norm at a time when in many
parishes it was regarded with suspicion. And I didn't experience a language barrier, since Greek and Latin were the
subjects I was studying—which led me to wonder why the
liturgy should be the private preserve of those with a
knowledge of dead languages.

It is in part a grateful return to my intermittent encounters with Anglican worship when I was a boy. None of
us in my family were ever communicant members of the
Church of England, but at one stage my mother dragged
us off regularly to morning or evening prayer in the village
church, and at around the same time—it was the early
years of the war—I was sent to an Anglican cathedral school.
This meant I automatically absorbed great chunks of the
psalms—Cranmer adapted the Anglican services of morning
and evening prayer from the Lauds and Vespers of the
Roman breviary, and each is built around two or three
psalms together with such canticles as the *Benedictus*, the

Magnificat, and the *Nunc dimittis.* And I was exposed to readings from both the Old and the New Testaments.

All this has left me with a vague familiarity with the Bible, a familiarity now reinforced by the readings at Sunday mass. It is at least a basis. But it's hardly good enough. As someone trying to be a Christian I should be soaked in the Bible, discovering in it that radical re-interpretation of human life which I then need to apply to the life that I am experiencing; not the discovery of another world but a radical transformation of this world which is able to give hope and meaning to precisely this world's concerns and anxieties. I should use odd moments of leisure to familiarize myself more deeply with what God was saying to his people of the old covenant through and in their very secular history, with what Jesus said and did and how disciples of his like the evangelists and Paul interpreted this in the light of their own experience and surroundings. And then I ought to ponder over all this and try to school myself to listen, to become more sensitive to what is going on around me and less insistent on making my own voice heard and on giving vent to my own private needs and quirks.

Here there's another difficulty I need to face up to. My whole approach is apt to be overintellectual. True, I dislike the label intellectual, and overexposure to intellectual small talk and nit-picking is apt to breed the same strong reaction as overexposure to spirituality. Perhaps it is that I'm an intellectual manqué. But, whatever label I like to pin on myself rather than face up to the implications of simply being human, with all the complexities that this entails, I tend to approach everything in an overintellectual and overrational manner.

This means that for me it's apt to be not so much a question of believing as scurrying around trying to find rational arguments for believing. To adapt a famous remark about metaphysics, it's finding bad reasons for what I ought to believe by instinct. I need to learn to trust my emotions and my instincts more. This doesn't mean giving way to credulity or sentimentality, but learning to accept the limitations of reason, realizing that this side of the kingdom we can never have a complete answer, that now we see through a glass darkly and only then face to face. It's a question of learning and practicing discernment, of recognizing which emotions and instincts mark an authentic response and which are somewhat less than human.

And this is where I find the label "spiritual life" unsatisfactory. I've used it out of mental laziness: I can't think of a more suitable term, though we badly need one, and the traditional connotation does at least provide a starting point. What is wrong with it is the implicaton that my spiritual life is somehow separate and distinct from the rest of my life, from my life in general. Inasmuch as I've got a spiritual life—and anyone who has read thus far will realize how dubious that claim is—then it's inseparable from the rest of my life. It's not me playing a different role from me as a husband, me as a father, me as a journalist. Rather it is, or it ought to be, the authentic me, a way of interpreting and understanding my life as a whole that gives meaning to this as I live it out in the different roles I am called on to fulfill. I'm not a spirit encased or entrapped in a body. I can't conceive of life without a body, and I don't think any Christian can—which is why in the creed we proclaim our faith in the resurrection of the body, which is another way of saying we trust in Jesus's promise that he came to give us life, and life more abundantly.

Perhaps we should talk, instead, of learning to live. It's a process we start on in the womb and must carry on with until death—for as soon as we stop learning to live, as soon as we close in on ourselves, we die, in the sense of giving up our hope in the resurrection. It means learning to live calmly among a network of tensions. We need to live in the moment, in the here and now, while at the same time being ready to welcome the future and to learn from (and not reject) the past. We need to accept the limitations placed upon us by our bodies, by being confined to one particular point in time and space, by the kind of people we are and the kind of surroundings we live in, while at the same time refusing to let these limitations dictate our choices and circumscribe our freedom. We need to be in but not of the world, fully involved in all the aspects of the life of our society, not blindly accepting its presuppositions and prejudices, but instead subjecting them to the radical critique of the Gospel.

Above all, it is learning to live with other people, accepting them as they are and not as we would like them to be so that they would fit in more easily with our private desires and fantasies. Again there's a tension, between the need not to exploit others and the need not to be exploited ourselves so that we get twisted away from the kind of person we are meant to be and the kind of contribution we should be making.

So I've outlined a program for myself, but how far I shall go toward realizing it is another matter. It's a question of probing continually for deeper understanding—of myself, of all the instincts and emotions and intellectual quirks that stop my being fully human; of other people, of their needs and their individuality and their point of view; and of the Gospel and its radical re-interpretaton of what the tragicomedy of human existence is all about. What I am intermittently in search of can best be described as an attitude of critical humility. And the means have to be the whole of my life.